COVER PHOTO: PESTO STUFFED CHERRY TOMATOES PAGE 81

ECLECTIC ENTERTAINING™

Published by:
eclectic-entertaining.com
eclecticentertaining@gmail.com

9876 Clairton Way
Highlands Ranch, CO 80126

First Printing August 2012
ISBN 9 780985788605
Library of Congress Control Number
2012913062

eclectic
ENTERTAINING

15 complete dinner party menus
for busy people who like to cook

barbara stafford

Forward

"If you can read you can cook!"

When my mother uttered those very words to my sister and me at very young ages, the mystery of cooking was immediately stripped away because we both could read. So obviously we could then learn to cook, which was our goal. The funny thing is that my mom was never an avid cook and kept meals pretty simple. After hearing those words come out of her mouth, I assumed the obvious – Mom can't read! Seriously, for years I believed that to be true until I was late in high school. When I divulged the secret I thought I had needed to keep, the laughter within the family exploded and continues to this day. My mom has a good sense of humor, thankfully!

On that note, I must thank my mother, Jean McCluskey, for giving me the courage to try new recipes, my dear father for encouraging me to keep writing as he loved eating (I regret that he did not live long enough to see it finished), my son Scott Mitchell, for giving me a deadline to finish it (his birthday!) and my daughter Kristin Mitchell, for giving me endless moral support in this endeavor. But this book would not have even happened had it not been for the vision of my wonderful husband, John, who thought I had a knack for putting together dinner party menus and grocery lists in a way others may use. We enjoy entertaining and hope other busy people will too, especially now that we have saved the cook time by already providing the complete menus and grocery lists. Sorry, you have to do the rest!

Barbara Stafford

Ec-lec-tic
choosing from several sources, selecting the best from each one, not following any one method

ACKNOWLEDGEMENTS

GRAPHIC DESIGN
Bill McConnell,
Rivet Designworks

PRINTING
Mike McCluskey,
Proforma SoCal

WEB DESIGN
Jim Lyons,
Websetter, LLC

PHOTOGRAPHY
John Stafford

PHOTO EDITOR
Laura Stafford

Contents

Beef yakitori k-bobs

MENU

Baba ghannooj (eggplant dip)

Shrimp with ginger-grilled pineapple

Couscous with chick peas and spinach

Beef yakitori k-bobs

Grilled broccoli

Orange pilaf

Apple puff pastry

Baba ghannooj (eggplant dip)

2 large eggplants

1 medium onion, cut in half

4 garlic cloves, crushed

3 lemons, juiced

¼ cup tahini (sesame seed paste)

2 tablespoons extra virgin olive oil

¼ teaspoon cumin

Salt to taste

Pita bread and vegetable dippers

In a 400 degree oven, bake eggplants about 40 minutes until soft. Cool, peel, cube. Place eggplant cubes, onion, garlic, lemon juice, tahini, olive oil, cumin and salt in food processor. Whirl until smooth. Taste, adjust salt. Serve at room temperature with pita bread and vegetable dippers.

GROCERY LIST	(QUANTITY)
FRESH	
Eggplant	2 large
Garlic cloves	4
Lemons	3
Onion	1 medium
Veggies dippers of choice (carrots, broccoli, snap peas, zucchini, cucumbers, etc.)	
CANS/JARS	
Olive oil. Extra virgin	2 T.
Tahini (Sesame seed paste), may be in foreign foods section or check health food store.	¼ cup
BAKING	
Cumin	¼ tsp.
Salt	to taste
MISC.	
Pita bread to dip Check bread or bakery area.	

Shrimp with ginger-grilled pineapple

1 T. extra virgin olive oil

32 oz. bag of frozen, uncooked, deveined shrimp, medium sized

Kosher salt and freshly ground pepper

1 medium onion, finely chopped

1 tsp. minced garlic

½ cup orange juice

¼ cup lime, squeezed

2 T. scallions, minced (green onion)

2 T. fresh cilantro, minced

1 ½ T. fresh ginger, minced

1 T. sesame oil

Salt and pepper to taste

1 pineapple, large, ripe, peeled, quartered lengthwise and cored

1 tsp. sesame seeds

Heat oil in large, nonstick pan. Season the shrimp with salt and pepper and cook over high heat for 1 minute. Add the onion and garlic and cook, stirring occasionally, until shrimp are cooked (pink) but not tough. Stir in the OJ, 2 T. of the lime juice, the green onions and cilantro. Transfer to a bowl and let cool.

(Continued on next page)

GROCERY LIST	(QUANTITY)
FRESH	
Cilantro	2 T.
Garlic	1 tsp. (~1 clove)
Ginger	1 ½ tsp.
Lime juice	¼ cup
Onion	1
Pineapple	1
Scallions	2 T.
CANS/JARS	
Olive oil Extra virgin	1 T.
Sesame oil	1 T.
DRY	
Kosher salt	
Pepper Freshly ground	
Sesame seeds	1 T.
DAIRY	
Orange juice Already made	½ cup
MEAT	
Shrimp Frozen, uncooked	32 oz.

In another bowl, combine remaining 2 T. lime juice, ginger, sesame oil, ½ tsp. salt and ¼ tsp. pepper. Brush the pineapple with the mixture and let stand at room temperature 30 min.

In a dry frying pan, toast sesame seeds over high heat, shaking pan and stirring about 2 minutes. Set aside until the end.

Grill or broil pineapple 2 minutes per side, turning once, until browned. Cut each quarter crosswise into ½" thick pieces and arrange on a large serving plate. Intermingle shrimp with pineapple slices and spoon OJ marinade over and sprinkle with the toasted sesame seeds. Serve with toothpicks and small appetizer plates.

Couscous with chick peas & spinach

10 oz. box couscous, plain

¼ cup + 1 T. extra virgin olive oil

1 tsp. salt

½ cup raisins or craisins

2 T. fresh lemon juice

2 large tomatoes, chopped

½ tsp. cumin seeds

1 large garlic clove, minced

6 oz. bag spinach

Zest of 1 lemon

15 oz. can chick peas, drained & rinsed

1 tsp. dried mint

Put couscous in glass or metal bowl, pour 1 ½ cups boiling water over, stir in ¼ cup oil & salt, covering with plate to sit for ten minutes.

Heat large skillet over medium heat, then toast cumin seeds for ~2 minutes. Add remaining 1 T. oil and garlic, sauté ~30 seconds. Add spinach and sauté until wilted. Fluff couscous with fork. Stir in raisins, lemon zest and lemon juice, pepper to taste. Fold in spinach, chick peas, mint and tomatoes. Serve warm or at room temperature.

GROCERY LIST	(QUANTITY)
FRESH	
Garlic clove	1
Lemon	1
Spinach	1
6 oz. bag baby spinach	
Tomatoes	2
CANS/JARS	
Chick peas.	1
15 oz. can (garbanzo beans)	
Olive oil. . . .	¼ cup + 1 T.
Extra virgin	
BAKING	
Cumin seeds.	½ tsp.
Mint	1 tsp.
Raisins or craisins . .	½ cup
Salt	1 tsp.
DRY	
Couscous	10 oz.
Plain	

Beef yakitori k-bobs

1 cup lite soy sauce

4 T. sesame oil

4 T. fresh lemon juice

2 T. sesame seeds

4 T. sugar

4 scallions, sliced thinly

2 cloves garlic, minced

2 tsp. fresh ginger, minced

2 pounds sirloin steak, cubed

Mix together in a medium bowl: soy, oil, lemon juice, sesame seeds, sugar, scallions, garlic and ginger. Add cubes of meat to marinade and allow to marinate overnight. Just before grilling, thread meat onto metal skewers. Heat grill, spray with nonstick spray, grill for approximately 10-15 minutes, turning a few times to cook evenly. Serves 8.

GROCERY LIST (QUANTITY)

FRESH

Garlic cloves 2
Ginger root . . . . . . .2 tsp.
Lemons 2
Scallions 4

CANS/JARS

Sesame oil . . . . .4 T.
Soy sauce . . . . 1 cup
Low sodium/lite

BAKING

Sesame seeds. . . . . . . 2 T.
Sugar . . . . 4 T.

MEAT

Sirloin steak . . . . . . .2 lbs.

Grilled broccoli

3 Large bunches of broccoli, washed with bottom end cut off

3 Lemons

Extra virgin olive oil

**Kosher salt
(optional, eliminate if on a low-salt diet)**

Gallon-sized zipper-type baggie

Cut broccoli lengthwise to include both flowers and stems. Place in gallon bag. Sprinkle with juiced lemon and enough olive oil to coat lightly. (The oil's purpose is to conduct heat during cooking as well as to add flavor.) Sprinkle with Kosher salt lightly. Place on sprayed grill and grill for ~2-3 minutes per side. Broccoli will appear slightly charred but not burned. If barbecuing is not an option, broil and it will be almost as good. Cut apart into serving sizes needed.

GROCERY LIST	(QUANTITY)
FRESH	
Broccoli	3
Large bunches	
Lemons	3
JARS/CANS	
Olive oil	
Extra virgin	
Cooking spray	
DRY	
Kosher salt	
Zipper-type baggie	1
Gallon size	

Orange pilaf

¼ cup butter

½ cup chopped celery

3 scallions, chopped

1 cup long-grain or basmati rice, uncooked

1 cup orange juice

1 tsp. salt

1 orange, peeled and chopped into small pieces

¼ cup almonds, slivered, toasted

In a large saucepan, sauté celery and scallions in butter until tender. Add the rice and brown lightly, stirring almost constantly. Add orange juice, salt and 1 cup water, heating to boiling. Reduce heat to simmer and cover for 25 minutes, until rice is tender and liquid has been absorbed. Stir in orange and almonds, serve. Serves 6-8.

GROCERY LIST (QUANTITY)

FRESH
Celery . . . . ½ cup
Orange 1
Scallions 3

DRY
Rice. . . . . 1 cup
Long-grain or basmati

BAKING
Almonds . . . . ¼ cup
Slivered

Salt . . . . .1 tsp.

DAIRY
Butter. . . . . . . ¼ cup (4 T.)
Orange juice . . . . . 1 cup

Apple puff pastry

3 large, firm apples, peeled and sliced
1/3 cup brown sugar
2 T. butter
½ cup walnuts, chopped
¼ tsp. cinnamon
½ lemon, juiced
4 ounces cream cheese, softened
2 T. sugar
¼ tsp. vanilla
1 egg, separated
½ package of frozen puff pastry, thawed

In a large frying pan, cook apples, brown sugar, butter, walnuts, cinnamon and lemon juice over medium heat until the apples are almost soft. Set aside and cool.

In a medium bowl, mix the cream cheese, sugar, vanilla and egg yolk. Set aside.

Cover a jellyroll pan with parchment paper. Set aside.

On a floured work surface, roll the puff pastry out until it is about a 12 x 10" rectangle. Place on the parchment paper/jellyroll pan. Spread the cream cheese mixture down the center third of the pastry. Place the apple mixture on top of

(Continued on next page)

GROCERY LIST	(QUANTITY)
FRESH	
Apples	3
(Granny Smith are good)	
Lemon	½
BAKING	
Brown sugar	1/3 cup
Cinnamon	¼ tsp.
Non-stick cooking spray	
Sugar	2 T.
Vanilla	¼ tsp.
Walnuts	½ cup
DAIRY	
Butter	2 T.
Cream cheese	4 oz.
Egg	1
FROZEN	
Puff pastry	½ box
MISC.	
Parchment paper	

the cream cheese. Now cut the sides of the pastry into one inch strips to fold over the apples. Beginning at one end, start folding the strips over, alternating sides to create a crisscross pattern. Pinch the very ends together so as to not lose the filling during baking.

Mix the egg white with 1 tsp. water and brush over the top and sides of pastry.

Bake at 375 degrees for 35 minutes until golden brown. Serves 6-8.

Grocery list BEEF YAKITORI K-BOBS MENU

FRESH

Apples 3
(Granny Smith are good)

Broccoli . . 3 large bunches

Celery . . . . ½ cup

Cilantro . . . . 2 T.

Eggplant . . . . . . 2 large

Garlic cloves 8

Ginger root . . . . 3½ tsp.

Lemons 9½

Lime juice . . . . ¼ cup

Onion 2

Orange 1

Pineapple 1

Scallions 9

Spinach 1
10 oz. bag, baby spinach

Tomatoes 2

Veggies dippers of choice
(carrots, broccoli, snap peas,
zucchini, cucumbers, etc.)

CANS/JARS

Chick peas 1
15 oz. can (garbanzo beans)

Olive oil . . . . . . ½ + cup
Extra virgin

Sesame oil . . . . 5 T.

Soy sauce . . . . . . 1 cup
Low sodium/lite

Tahini . . . . ¼ cup
(Sesame seed paste); may
be in foreign foods section

DRY

Couscous 1
10 oz. plain box

Rice . . . . 1 cup
Long-grain or basmati

BAKING

Almonds, slivered . . ¼ cup

Brown sugar . . . . . 1/3 cup

Cinnamon . . . . ¼ tsp.

cumin seeds . . . . . . ½ tsp.

Cumin, ground . . . . ¼ tsp.

Kosher salt

Mint . . . . 1 tsp.

Non-stick cooking spray

Pepper
Freshly ground

Raisins or Craisins . . ½ cup

Salt . . . . 2+ tsp.

Sesame seeds . . . . 3 T.

Sugar . . . . 6 T.

Vanilla . . . . ¼ tsp.

Walnuts . . . . ½ cup

DAIRY

Butter . . . . 6 T.

Cream cheese . . . . . 4 oz.

Egg 1

Orange juice . . . 1½ cups
Already made, from concentrate

MEAT

Shrimp . . . . . 32 oz. bag
Frozen, uncooked, deveined,
medium sized

Sirloin steak . . . . 2 lbs.

FROZEN

Puff pastry . . . . ½ box

MISC.

Parchment paper

Pita bread to dip
Check bread or bakery area

Zipper-type baggie 1
Gallon size

Braised chicken

Prosciutto bundles

Cranberry crostini

Waldorf salad

Braised chicken

Spinach stuffed tomatoes

Lemon and mint orzo with peas

Carrot cake with cream cheese frosting

MENU

Prosciutto bundles

12 slices Prosciutto

4 ounces ricotta cheese, fresh

4 ounces goat cheese, soft

½ lemon zested

1 T. basil, minced (fresh)

1 tsp. parsley, minced

Peppercorns

1 ripe pear, apple or sun dried tomatoes, slivered into ~1 inch pieces

Cut Prosciutto into rectangles as much as possible.

Mix the 2 cheeses, zest, basil, parsley and peppercorns thoroughly. Into the center of a piece of Prosciutto, place about a ½ tsp. of cheese mixture. Add either a sliver of pear, apple or tomato. Roll up, then twist the ends to resemble a piece of wrapped candy. Chill before serving.

Cranberry crostini

1 Baguette, sliced into ¼" slices
4 T. walnut oil
½ cup walnuts, toasted and chopped
8 ounces blue cheese crumbles
2 T. shallots, minced
1/3 cup dried cranberries

Preheat oven to 400 degrees F. Place slices of bread on baking sheet, then brush with walnut oil. Bake until toasted, about 5 minutes.

Mix walnuts, cheese, shallots and cranberries in a bowl. Place a dollop onto each bread slice. Bake until cheese begins to melt, about 4 minutes.

Leftover tip: you may find that there is more topping than bread. Therefore, I recommend using the extra topping on pasta for another evening's dinner. Serve with green salad.

GROCERY LIST	(QUANTITY)
FRESH	
Shallots	2 T.
CANS/JARS	
Walnut oil	4 T.
DRY	
Baguette	1
BAKING	
Cranberries	1/3 cup
Dried	
Walnuts	½ cup
DAIRY	
Blue cheese	8 oz.
Crumbled	

Waldorf salad

1 cup light mayonnaise
¼ cup fresh lemon juice
3 red apples, firm, washed
2 cups celery, diced small
1 cup walnuts, toasted and chopped
¾ cup raisins
5 ounce bag of mixed greens

Mix together mayonnaise and lemon juice. Dice apples into small cubes and add to mayonnaise, coating well. Add celery, walnuts and raisins, blend. Arrange 8 salad plates with greens as a base, then spoon salad into center of each. Serves 8.

GROCERY LIST	(QUANTITY)
FRESH	
Apples	3
Red, firm ones	
Celery	2 cups
Chopped	
Lemon	1
Mixed greens	1
5 oz. bag	
CANS/JARS	
Mayonnaise	1 cup
Light	
BAKING	
Raisins	¾ cup
Walnuts	1 cup
Chopped	

Braised chicken

5 lbs. chicken breasts, skinned and boned

1 head garlic

¼ cup dry oregano

Pepper, freshly ground to taste

½ cup red wine vinegar

½ cup extra virgin olive oil

1 cup prunes, pitted

½ cup Spanish (green) olives, stuffed with pimentos

½ cup capers, small ones, 3.5 oz. jar

6 bay leaves

Mix all of the above ingredients and marinate overnight in a covered dish or bowl.

Place chicken and all above ingredients in a 9 x13" Pyrex dish, heating oven to 350 degrees.

Mix below ingredients and pour over chicken:

1 cup brown sugar

1 cup white table wine

Braise in oven for 50 – 60 minutes, until chicken is no longer pink. If possible, use a remote control meat thermometer to cook perfectly. Serves 8 hungry people.

GROCERY LIST	(QUANTITY)
FRESH	
1 head of garlic	
CANS/JARS	
Capers	3.5 oz. jar
Green olives	½ cup
Olive oil	½ cup
Extra virgin	
Red wine vinegar	½ cup
White wine	1 cup
BAKING	
Bay leaves	6
Brown sugar	1 cup
Oregano	¼ cup
Pepper	to taste
Freshly ground	
Prunes	1 cup
Pitted	
MEAT	
Chicken breasts	5 lbs.
Skinned & boned	

Spinach stuffed tomatoes

8 medium tomatoes
2 T. butter
1/8 cup Italian flavored bread crumbs
½ cup cooked rice, any kind
¼ cup chicken broth, low sodium
½ lemon, juiced
6 scallions, sliced
2 garlic cloves, minced
10 ounces frozen spinach, thawed and drained
½ tsp. oregano
¼ tsp. nutmeg, thyme and white pepper
Freshly ground peppercorns
1/3 cup fresh Pecorino Romano cheese, grated

Wash tomatoes and dry, then slice off the top ¼ and set aside. Scoop out insides, reserve for another recipe, and flip over to drain on paper towels.

Chop up 2 of the tomato tops and put into a saucepan with 2 T. butter. Add bread crumbs, rice, broth, lemon juice, scallions, garlic, spinach, oregano, nutmeg, thyme, white pepper and freshly ground pepper. Cook until warm and blended. Remove from heat and add cheese. Fill all the tomatoes and then bake at 350 degrees 25-30 minutes, until heated thoroughly. Serves 8.

GROCERY LIST	(QUANTITY)
FRESH	
Garlic cloves	2
Lemon	½
Scallions	6
Tomatoes Medium	8
CANS/JARS	
Chicken broth Low sodium	¼ cup
DRY	
Bread crumbs Italian flavored	1/8 cup
Rice. Uncooked, any kind	¼ cup
BAKING	
Nutmeg	¼ tsp.
Oregano	½ tsp.
Peppercorns	to taste
Thyme	¼ tsp.
White pepper	¼ tsp.
DAIRY	
Butter	2 T.
Romano cheese Fresh, grated	1/3 cup
FROZEN	
Spinach Chopped	10 oz.

Lemon & mint orzo with peas

2 cups uncooked orzo

1 ½ cup frozen peas, thawed

3 T. butter

2 lemons, juiced

Zest of one lemon

2 T. fresh mint leaves, minced

Prepare orzo according to directions on package, drain. Return to warm pan and add peas, butter, lemon juice and zest. Mix well until warmed throughout, turning burner back on if necessary. Gently mix in mint. 8 servings

GROCERY LIST	(QUANTITY)
FRESH	
Lemons	2
Mint	2 T.
DRY	
Orzo	2 cups
(Near the pasta section)	
DAIRY	
Butter	3 T.
FROZEN	
Peas	1 ½ cup

Carrot cake with cream cheese frosting

CAKE

1 ½ cups vegetable oil

2 cups sugar

4 eggs

2 cups flour
(in Denver, high altitude, add 2 T. more flour)

1 tsp salt

2 tsp baking soda

2 tsp cinnamon

3 cups finely grated carrots (1 pound)

½ cup finely chopped pecans

½ cup golden raisins

FROSTING

8 oz. package of cream cheese, soft

½ cup (1 stick) butter, soft

2 tsp vanilla

4 ½ cups (1 pound) powdered sugar

GROCERY LIST	(QUANTITY)
FRESH	
Carrots . . . . 1 lb.	
(3 cups grated)	
CANS/JARS	
Vegetable oil . . . 1½ cups	
DAIRY	
Cream cheese . . . . . 8 oz.	
Butter. . . . . ½ cup	
Eggs 4	
BAKING	
Baking soda . . . . . . .2 tsp.	
Cinnamon . . . . .2 tsp.	
Flour . . . . .2 cups	
(+ 2 T., possibly)	
Pecans. . . . . ½ cup	
Golden raisins . . . . ½ cup	
Salt . . . . .1 tsp.	
Sugar . . . . .2 cups	
Powdered sugar . . . . 1 lb.	
(4 ½ cups)	
Vanilla. . . . . .2 tsp.	

Preheat oven to 350 degrees. Grease and sugar a bundt cake pan. In a large bowl with an electric mixer, blend oil and sugar. Beat in eggs 1 at a time. In a separate bowl blend together flour, salt, baking soda and cinnamon. Add to batter and mix well. Stir in carrots, pecans and raisins. Pour batter into prepared pan. Bake at 35 minutes (55 minutes in Denver) or until toothpick inserted comes out clean. Cool cake, remove from pan and frost with cream cheese frosting. Chill until ready to serve.

(Continued on next page)

In medium bowl, beat cream cheese, butter and vanilla with electric mixer. Gradually add sugar and beat until smooth. Recipe is generous so you may end up freezing some of it... personal choice! Spread desired amount over bundt cake.

Grocery list  BRAISED CHICKEN MENU

FRESH

1 head of garlic + 2 cloves
Apples. 3
Red, firm ones

Basil . . . . .1 T.
Carrots . . . . 1 lb.
(3 cups grated)

Celery . . . . .2 cups
Chopped

Lemons 4
Mint . . . . .2 T.
Mixed greens . . 5 oz. bag
Parsley. . . . . .1 tsp.
Pear or apple 1
Scallions 6
Shallots . . . . .2 T.
Tomatoes Medium 8

CANS/JARS

Capers . . . . . .3.5 oz. jar
Chicken broth. . . . . ¼ cup
Low sodium

Olive oil. . . . . ½ cup
Extra virgin

Green olives. . . . . . ½ cup
Mayonnaise . . 1 cup, light
Red wine vinegar . . ½ cup
Sun dried tomatoes 1
Small jar (if not using
pear or apple)

Vegetable oil . . . 1½ cups
Walnut oil . . . . .4 T.

DRY

Baguette 1
Bread crumbs . . . .1/8 cup
Italian flavored

Orzo . . . . .2 cups
(Near the pasta)

Rice. . . . . ¼ cup
Uncooked, any kind

MEAT/DELI

Chicken breast . . . . .5 lbs.
Skinned & boned

Prosciutto . . . . . 12 slices
Not too thin if having cut by a
butcher or they will fall apart
when working with them.

FROZEN

Peas . . . . 1½ cup
Spinach . . . . .10 oz.
Chopped

DAIRY

Blue cheese . . . . . . .8 oz.
Crumbled

Butter. . . . . 13 T.
Cream cheese . . . .8 oz.
Eggs 4
Goat cheese. . . . . . .4 oz.
Soft

Ricotta cheese. . . . . .4 oz.
Fresh

Romano cheese . .1/3 cup
Fresh, grated

BAKING

Baking soda. . . . . . .2 tsp.
Bay leaves 6
Brown sugar. . . . . . 1 cup
Cinnamon . . . . .2 tsp.
Cranberries Dried. .1/3 cup
Flour . . . . .2 cups
(Plus 2 T., possibly)

Golden raisins . . . . ½ cup
Nutmeg . . . . ¼ tsp.
Oregano . ¼ cup + ½ tsp.
Pecans. . . . . ½ cup
Peppercorns . . . . . to taste
In 3 recipes

Powdered sugar . . . . 1 lb.
(4 ½ cups)

Prunes Pitted . . . . . . 1 cup
Raisins. . . . . ¾ cup
Salt . . . . .1 tsp.
Sugar . . . . .2 cups
Thyme . . . . ¼ tsp.
Vanilla. . . . . .2 tsp.
Walnuts . . . . 1½ cup
Chopped

White pepper. . . . . . ¼ tsp.

MISC.

White wine . . . . . . 1 cup

Cajun-inspired chicken

Cherry tomato-mozzarella-basil k-bobs

Pear-gorgonzola-caramelized onion cups

Pear, pecan & mixed greens salad

Cajun-inspired chicken

Broiled asparagus

Polenta

Chocolate stuffed pears in puff pastry

Cherry tomato-mozzarella-basil k-bobs

Cherry tomatoes, washed

Fresh mozzarella cheese, sliced into cubes close to the size of the tomatoes

Fresh basil leaves, separated

Round toothpicks

Skewer onto each toothpick: one tomato, piece of cheese and one leaf of basil. Either lay skewers on serving plate or poke into lettuce-covered styrofoam half-ball, as seen in photo.

GROCERY LIST (QUANTITY)

FRESH

Cherry tomatoes 1
Container

Fresh mozzarella cheese
Container, in deli near produce in most grocery stores.

Fresh basil leaves
(Buy the entire plant if possible, and grow in sunny spot in kitchen. This is so handy to have!)

DRY

Round toothpicks. . . 1 box

MISC.

Styrofoam
(Half) ball found at craft store

Pear-gorgonzola-caramelized onion cups

1 medium onion, sliced thinly and then chopped

1 tsp. + 1/2 tsp. butter

½ tsp. sugar

Dash salt, optional

½ tsp. balsamic vinegar

15 prepared filo dough shells

½ pear, peeled and chopped

3 ounces gorgonzola cheese, crumbled

First, caramelize onion by cooking it in a frying pan with 1 tsp. butter over medium-high heat for ten minutes. Let the onion brown but not burn, turning occasionally. After ten minutes, add sugar and salt, lower heat to low-medium, cooking another ten minutes. Then add ½ tsp. butter and cook ten more minutes, a total of 30 minutes. Then turn heat off and add balsamic vinegar, stirring to coat onions in it. Set aside and prepare below:

Next, line a baking dish with the filo shells. Fill bottoms with cheese, then pear, then top with onions. Bake at 350 degrees for 7 minutes, serve hot

Leftover tip – there may be excess onions. Toss them into any vegetable dish, pasta or eat alone and they will not disappoint!

GROCERY LIST	(QUANTITY)
FRESH	
Onion	1
Medium	
Pear	½
CANS/JARS	
Balsamic vinegar	½ tsp.
BAKING	
Salt	dash
Sugar	½ tsp.
DAIRY	
Butter	1½ tsp.
Gorgonzola cheese	3 oz.
FROZEN	
Filo dough shells	1 box
Prepared	

Pear, pecan & mixed greens salad

10 ounces mixed greens

2 medium pears, ripe

1 cup seedless red grape halves

1 cup Ranch Dressing (light or regular)

Mix the above ingredients in a large salad bowl. Toss.

1/3 cup pecans, toasted

4 ounces Blue cheese

Plate the salads and top with pecans and blue cheese.

Cajun-inspired chicken

12 bacon strips, diced

1 cup butter

4 garlic cloves, minced

4 T. Old Bay seafood seasoning

4 T. Dijon mustard

1 T. chili powder

2 tsp. pepper

2 tsp. Louisiana-style hot sauce

½ tsp. basil, dry

½ tsp. oregano

½ tsp. thyme

2 pounds chicken tenders, uncooked

Cook bacon in a large frying pan until mostly cooked, then drain and return bacon to pan. Add all remaining ingredients EXCEPT chicken, cooking over low heat about five minutes. Preheat oven to 375 degrees.

Place chicken in 9x12" glass baking dish. Pour sauce over all evenly. Bake uncovered for 20-25 minutes, stirring twice. Serves 8.

GROCERY LIST	(QUANTITY)
FRESH	
Garlic cloves	4
CANS/JARS	
Dijon mustard	4 T.
Hot sauce.	2 tsp.
Louisiana-style	
BAKING	
Basil	½ tsp.
Chili powder	1 T.
Seafood seasoning . . .	4 T.
Old Bay brand	
Oregano	½ tsp.
Peppercorns	2 tsp.
Thyme	½ tsp.
DAIRY	
Butter.	1 cup
MEAT	
Bacon	12 slices
Chicken tenders	2 lbs.

Broiled asparagus

2 large bundles asparagus, washed with ends cut off

¼ cup extra virgin olive oil

1 tsp. lemon pepper

¼ tsp. garlic powder

½ tsp. sea or kosher salt

Into a large zipper-type baggie, place all the ingredients and toss until well-coated. Place in refrigerator until needed. Preheat broiler and place oven rack directly under broiler. Place asparagus on broiler pan, place in oven and broil for a minute, turn over, checking after another minute. Broil until al dente or cooked to personal preference. This may also be done on a grill. Serves 8.

GROCERY LIST	(QUANTITY)
FRESH	
Asparagus	2 bundles
CANS/JARS	
Olive oil	¼ cup
Extra virgin	
BAKING	
Garlic powder	¼ tsp.
Lemon pepper	1 tsp.
Sea or kosher salt	½ tsp.
MISC.	
Zipper-type plastic bags	
Gallon size	

Polenta

6 ½ cups chicken broth, low sodium, MSG-free
2 tsp. salt
1 ½ cups polenta or coarse, yellow cornmeal
2 T. butter

Bring broth to a boil in a large pot and add the salt. Slowly add the cornmeal/polenta to the water, stirring constantly into the boiling liquid. Reduce to a medium heat and cook until thick and not grainy, about 30-40 minutes, stirring occasionally. Add butter and serve immediately. Serves 8.

GROCERY LIST	(QUANTITY)

CANS/JARS
Chicken broth . . . 6½ cups
Low sodium, MSG-free

DRY
Polenta . . . . 1½ cups
Or coarse, yellow cornmeal
Salt . . . . .2 tsp.

DAIRY
Butter. . . . . .2 T.

Chocolate stuffed pears in puff pastry

8 medium pears, ripe
~ ¾ cup semi sweet chocolate chips
¼ cup milk
1 17.4 oz. package Puff Pastry Sheets, thawed
Flour

Chocolate sauce - for ice cream sundaes
Caramel sauce - for ice cream sundaes
Fresh mint leaves for garnish

Carefully peel pears leaving stems attached. Cut tops off about 1/3 down, toward thickest part of pear. Scoop out core, being careful not to break through bottom. Fill cavity with chocolate chips and replace top.

Spread thawed puff pastry flat on floured pastry sheet. Roll flat with rolling pin. Cut each rectangle into four squares, totaling 8 pastry squares. Place one pear in the middle of each pastry square, pulling the sides up around the fruit and covering it, leaving stem exposed. With wet hands, press dough tightly around pear and smooth out seams as much as possible. Brush with milk. Can be made a day ahead and covered in plastic wrap.

Heat oven to 425 degrees. Place pears on ungreased, glass

(Continued on next page)

GROCERY LIST	(QUANTITY)
FRESH	
Mint leaves	~8
For garnish	
Pears	8
Medium	
CANS/JARS	
Caramel sauce	
(May be near ice cream)	
Chocolate sauce	
(May be near ice cream)	
BAKING	
Chocolate chips . .	12 oz. bag
Flour	for dusting
DAIRY	
Milk	¼ cup
FROZEN	
Puff Pastry Sheets . .	1 box

baking dish and bake 15 minutes. Reduce temperature to
375 degrees and bake 10 minutes longer, browning pastry.

Drizzle caramel and chocolate sauces decoratively on plate
and place pear on top. Garnish plate with fresh mint sprig.
Serves 8.

Grocery list

FRESH

Asparagus . . . . . 2 bundles
Cherry tomatoes 1
Container

Fresh basil leaves
(Buy the entire plant if possible,
and grow in sunny spot in kitchen.
This is so handy to have!)

Fresh mozzarella cheese
Container, in deli near produce
in most grocery stores.

Garlic cloves 4
Mint leaves . . . . ~8 leaves
For garnish

Mixed greens . . . . . 10 oz.
Onion 1
Medium

Pears 10½
Medium, ripe

Red grapes . . . . . . 1 cup
Seedless

CANS/JARS

Balsamic vinegar . . . ½ tsp.
Caramel sauce
(may be near ice cream)

Chicken broth . . . 6½ cups
Low sodium, MSG-free

Chocolate sauce
(May be near ice cream)

Dijon mustard . . . . . . 4 T.
Olive oil
Extra virgin

Hot sauce . . . . 2 tsp.
Louisiana-style

Salad dressing . . . . . . 1 cup
Ranch style, light or regular

DRY

Polenta . . . . 1½ cups
Or coarse, yellow cornmeal

BAKING

Basil . . . . ½ tsp.
Chili powder . . . . 1 T.
Chocolate chips 1
12 oz. bag

Flour . . . . for dusting
Garlic powder . . . . ¼ tsp.
Lemon pepper . . . . . . 1 tsp.
Seafood seasoning . . . 4 T.
Old Bay brand

Oregano . . . . ½ tsp.
Pecans . . . . 1/3 cup
Whole

Peppercorns . . . . 2 tsp.
Salt . . . . 2 tsp. + dash
Sea or kosher salt . . ½ tsp.
Sugar . . . . ½ tsp.
Thyme . . . . ½ tsp.

DAIRY

Blue cheese . . . . . . 4 oz.
(May be in deli)

Butter . . . . . 1 cup + 2½ T.
Gorgonzola cheese . . 3 oz.
(May be in deli)

Milk . . . . ¼ cup

MEAT

Bacon . . . . 12 slices
Chicken tenders . . . . 2 lbs.

FROZEN

Filo dough shells . . 1 box
Prepared

Puff Pastry Sheets . . 1 box

MISC.

Round toothpicks . . . 1 box
Zipper-type plastic bags
Gallon size

Chicken breasts stuffed with spinach, blue cheese, bacon & craisins

MENU

Tomato crostini

Baked apples, rosemary and brie

Walnut, gruyere and greens salad

Chicken breasts stuffed with spinach,
blue cheese, bacon and craisins

Grilled beets

Almond and poppy seed pasta

Mexican wedding cakes

Chocolate brandy truffles

Tomato crostini

6 on-the-vine tomatoes, chopped

½ cup sun-dried tomatoes, chopped

4 garlic cloves, minced

½ tsp. oregano

**¼ cup extra virgin olive oil
+ enough for brushing on baguettes**

2 tablespoons aged balsamic vinegar

**¼ cup packed fresh basil,
"chopped" with kitchen shears**

Pinch salt

Ground pepper

2 baguettes cut into ½" slices

¾ cup mozzarella cheese, grated

Heat oven to 350 degrees. Brush both sides of bread with olive oil, place on baking sheet and toast for 8 minutes. Remove from oven.

Mix together: fresh tomatoes, sun-dried tomatoes, garlic, oregano, ¼ cup olive oil, balsamic vinegar, basil, salt and pepper to taste. May be made in advance to allow flavors to blend.

Spoon tomato mixture on top of toasted bread, sprinkle cheese over top. Return to oven and bake 5 minutes or until cheese melts, serve warm.

GROCERY LIST	(QUANTITY)
FRESH	
Basil	¼ cup
Packed	
Garlic cloves	4
Tomatoes	6
On-the-vine	
CANS/JARS	
Olive oil	¼ cup+
Extra virgin	
Balsamic vinegar	2 T.
Aged	
Sun dried tomatoes	½ cup
DRY	
Baguettes	2
BAKING	
Oregano	½ tsp.
Pepper	
Salt	
DAIRY	
Mozzarella cheese	¾ cup
Grated	

Baked apples, rosemary and brie

4 large, tart apples, preferably both green and red, if possible, sliced thick and cut in half
16 ounces brie, cut into small pieces
Peppercorns
Fresh rosemary sprigs, chopped
Crackers

In an ovenproof dish, spread apples evenly over bottom. Spread brie evenly over top of apples, then grind fresh peppercorns over brie, then sprinkle rosemary over all, lightly. Bake at 350 for ten minutes or until cheese melts. Serve with crackers and a wide knife for scooping up apples and spreading onto cracker.

GROCERY LIST (QUANTITY)

FRESH
Apples. 4
Large tart, red and green

Rosemary. . . . . . . 1 bunch

BAKING
Peppercorns

DAIRY
Brie. . . . . 16 oz.
(May be in deli)

DRY
Crackers
Any kind

Walnut, gruyere and greens salad

¼ cup extra virgin olive oil

2 T. balsamic vinegar

1 T. Dijon mustard

¼ tsp. sugar

½ tsp. salt

½ tsp. Freshly ground pepper

10 ounces mixed salad greens

½ cup sliced red cabbage

½ cup walnuts, toasted and chopped

6 ounces Gruyere cheese, cut into thin strips (or substitute any hard, nutty cheese)

Make dressing by combining oil, vinegar, mustard, sugar, salt and pepper, blending well. In large salad bowl, combine salad greens, cabbage, walnuts and cheese. Toss with dressing right before serving. 8 servings.

GROCERY LIST	(QUANTITY)
FRESH	
Mixed greens	1
10 oz. bag	
Red cabbage	1
Small	
CANS/JARS	
Balsamic vinegar	2 T.
Dijon mustard	1 T.
Olive oil	¼ cup
Extra virgin	
BAKING	
Peppercorns	½ tsp
Sugar	¼ tsp.
Salt	½ tsp.
Walnuts	½ cup
DAIRY	
Gruyere cheese	6 oz.
(Or other hard, nutty cheese; may be in deli)	

Chicken breasts stuffed with spinach, blue cheese, bacon and craisins

8 chicken breasts, boned and skinned

8 slices bacon, uncooked

Salt & pepper

1/2 cup flour

20 oz. frozen spinach, thawed and drained

1 cup blue cheese, crumbled

1 cup craisins (dried cranberries)

In a medium skillet, fry bacon until crispy, remove from pan and drain on paper towels, reserving bacon drippings. Break bacon into small pieces when cool enough to handle. Slice chicken breasts horizontally but not entirely through, enabling them to be opened flat and doubling their size. Place the breasts on a floured board using the ¼ cup flour sprinkled underneath the chicken. Pound each breast until half the thickness, then salting and peppering them.

In a bowl, mix bacon crumbs, spinach, blue cheese and craisins until blended. Place ¼ of the amount on each breast. Roll breasts tightly until all the filling has been secured inside, using toothpicks to hold together.

Heat the bacon drippings and then sear the chicken quickly to just brown and seal in the flavors. Then transfer chicken to an ovenproof dish and bake at 350 degrees for 20 minutes. Check to be sure all pink is gone, serve. Serves 8.

GROCERY LIST	(QUANTITY)
BAKING	
Dried cranberries	1 cup
Flour	½ cup
Salt and pepper	to taste
DAIRY	
Blue cheese	1 cup
Crumbled	
MEAT	
Bacon	8 slices
Chicken	8 breasts
Boned and skinned	
FROZEN	
Spinach	20 oz.

Grilled beets

16 Fresh beets – allow 2 per person
Extra virgin olive oil
Salt
Pepper
Aluminum foil
Aged balsamic vinegar

Cut greens from beets, then peel beets and wash greens until clean. Reserve greens for later use.* Place beets on foil strip (that is long enough to fold over and close up) after spreading oil onto the foil, enough for each beet to sit in a small puddle of oil. Sprinkle with salt and pepper. Seal sides and close top of foil. Place on grill on medium heat for 30 minutes until tender. Slice and serve on a bed of spinach or on the beet greens. Drizzle aged balsamic vinegar over top and serve. Serves 8.

GROCERY LIST (QUANTITY)

FRESH
Beets 16
Allow 2 per person

CANS/JARS
Olive oil
Extra virgin
Aged balsamic vinegar

BAKING
Salt and Pepper

MISC.
Aluminum foil

*Beet greens may be used like lettuce for a salad or like spinach, cooked. They are very fibrous, dark green and loaded with iron! Beets are high in antioxidants, vitamin C and fiber.

Another tip is to peel the beets a day before entertaining as they will stain hands red!

Almond and poppy seed pasta

8 oz. box penne pasta or fettuccine
¼ cup butter
1 T. poppy seeds
½ cup almond slices, toasted

Cook pasta in salted, boiling water until al dente, drain well and place in large bowl. In small saucepan, melt butter. Add poppy seeds and stir until butter just begins to brown. Add to pasta, then add almonds and toss. Serves 6-8

GROCERY LIST	(QUANTITY)

DRY
Pasta of choice . . . . . 8 oz.
Recommend: penne or fettuccine

BAKING
Poppy seeds . . . . 1 T.
Slivered almonds . . ½ cup

DAIRY
Butter . . . . ¼ cup

Mexican wedding cakes (cookies)

½ lb. butter, softened

2 cups flour

1 cup almonds, chopped in food processor

½ cup powdered sugar

1 tsp. vanilla

Mix the above together and roll into small balls. Bake at 325 degrees for 15 minutes. Remove from oven, cool only very slightly and then remove from baking pan and roll in powdered sugar. Cool on cooling rack next. Nice and light little cookies.

GROCERY LIST (QUANTITY)

BAKING
Almonds . . . . 1 cup
Flour . . . . .2 cups
Powdered sugar . . . ½ cup
Vanilla. . . . . .1 tsp.

DAIRY
Butter. . . . . .½ lb.

Chocolate brandy truffles

12 ounces German sweet chocolate

¼ cup butter

¾ cup whipping cream, scalded

1 ½ T. brandy

Powdered sugar

12 ounces semisweet chocolate chips

Melt German chocolate with butter over a double boiler. Slowly strain scalded cream into double boiler with chocolate, ¼ cup at a time, whisking after each addition. Next, add the brandy and whisk well until smooth. Remove from heat, cover and refrigerate until firm, at least 2 hours.

Line a baking sheet with waxed paper. Using a small scoop (slightly larger than a melon baller), scoop chocolate and place on waxed paper, not worrying about a perfect shape at this point. Place back in refrigerator for 30 minutes or until firm.

Remove from fridge, cover palms of hands with powdered sugar and quickly roll each scoop of chocolate into a ball, replacing onto waxed paper and placing in freezer this time until firm.

Melt chocolate chips in a double boiler. Line another baking sheet with waxed paper. Working with about ten truffles at a time, remove from freezer, dip using two short skewers to manipulate them and cover completely, shaking off excess. Place on waxed paper, return to fridge until ten more are ready to join them. Repeat until all are dipped. Once firm, place each truffle in a paper candy cup and store in air-tight container until ready to use. Keep cold until ready to serve. Makes 3 dozen.

GROCERY LIST (QUANTITY)

BAKING
German chocolate . . . 12 oz.
Powdered sugar . . . ~¼ cup
Chocolate chips . . . 12 oz.
Semi sweet

DAIRY
Butter . . . . ¼ cup
Whipping cream . . . ¾ cup

MISC.
Brandy . . . . 1 ½ T.

German chocolate has nothing to do with the country – it is named after a man, John German.

Grocery list  CHICKEN BREASTS STUFFED WITH SPINACH MENU

FRESH

Apples 4
Large tart, red and green

Basil . . . . ¼ cup
Packed

Beets 16
Allow 2 per person

Garlic cloves 4

Mixed salad greens. . . . 1
10 oz. bag

Red cabbage . . . . 1 small

Rosemary. . . . . . . 1 bunch

Tomatoes 6
On-the-vine

CANS/JARS

Balsamic vinegar . . 4 + T.
Aged

Dijon mustard . . . . 1 T.

Olive oil. . . . . . . 1½ cups
Extra virgin

Sun dried tomatoes . . ½ cup

DRY

Baguettes 2

Crackers . . . . 1 box
Any kind

Pasta of choice . . . . . 8 oz.
Recommend penne or fettuccine

BAKING

Almonds . . . . 1 cup
Whole

Almonds . . . . ½ cup
Slivered

Dried Cranberries . . 1 cup

Flour . . . . 2½ cups

German chocolate . . . 12 oz.

Oregano . . . . ½ tsp.

Peppercorns . . . . . ½ + tsp

Poppyseeds . . . . 1 T.

Powdered sugar . . . ¾ cup

Salt . . . . ½ + tsp.

Chocolate chips . . . 12 oz.
Semi sweet

Sugar . . . . ¼ tsp.

Vanilla . . . . 1 tsp.

Walnuts . . . . ½ cup

DAIRY

Blue cheese . . . . . . 1 cup
Crumbled (check deli)

Brie . . . . 16 oz.
(May be in deli)

Butter . . . . 1½ cups

Gruyere cheese . . . . 6 oz.
(Or other hard, nutty
cheese; may be in deli)

Mozzarella cheese . . . ¾ cup
Grated

Whipping cream . . . ¾ cup

MEAT

Bacon . . . . 8 slices

Chicken . . . . 8 breasts
Boned and skinned

FROZEN

Spinach . . . . 20 oz.

MISC.

Aluminum foil

Brandy . . . . 1½ T.

Grilled scallops w/ lime sauce

MENU

Artichoke, tomato and mozzarella boats

Bacon-wrapped water chestnuts

Hearty spinach salad with vinaigrette

Grilled scallops with lime sauce

Phyllo-wrapped asparagus

Saffron wild rice pilaf

Chocolate orange biscotti

Artichoke, tomato and mozzarella boats

1 14-ounce can artichoke bottoms in water, drained

Sun dried tomatoes, pieces

1 8-ounce container fresh mozzarella cheese

1 6-ounce container pesto

Drain artichoke bottoms, rinse and dry. Spread onto large baking sheet, open side facing up. Trim bottoms if necessary to make them sit level. Layer a small piece of mozzarella cheese (~1/2 tsp.), a dollop of pesto and a piece of tomato into artichoke bottom. Bake at 350 degrees for 6 minutes, just long enough to warm them up and melt cheese a little. Place on serving dish while still warm. Serve with small plates and forks.

GROCERY LIST	(QUANTITY)
CANS/JARS	
Artichoke bottoms 14 oz. can, in water	1
Sun dried tomatoes Small jar	1
DAIRY	
Basil Pesto Container	6 oz.
Mozzarella cheese Fresh; 8 oz. container	1

Bacon-wrapped water chestnuts

1 pound bacon
2 5-ounce cans water chestnuts, whole, drained
½ cup brown sugar
Soy sauce, optional

Cut bacon pieces in half and separate them. Cover both sides of the bacon pieces with the brown sugar. Roll one water chestnut up inside a piece of bacon, secure with a toothpick. Repeat until all the bacon is used. Drizzle soy sauce over tops, if desired. Place on broiler pan and bake 30 minutes at 350 degrees. Then broil briefly to brown bacon – watch very carefully! Serve hot.

GROCERY LIST	(QUANTITY)
CANS/JARS	
Soy sauce	optional
Enough to drizzle over all	
Water Chestnuts	2
5-oz. cans, whole	
BAKING	
Brown sugar	½ cup
MEAT	
Bacon	1 lb.
Uncooked, not microwave variety	
MISC.	
Round toothpicks	1 box

Hearty spinach salad with vinaigrette

10 ounces baby spinach, prewashed
4 ounces water chestnuts, diced
2 eggs, hardboiled and diced
½ cup bean sprouts
¼ pound bacon, crisp and crumbled
½ cup mushrooms, sliced
¼ red onion, diced

Mix the above ingredients in a large salad bowl. Mix dressing (below) and toss with salad just before serving.

¼ cup canola oil
¼ cup red wine vinegar
1 T. sugar
¼ cup ketchup
Dash of soy sauce
1 garlic clove, minced

Mix vinaigrette ingredients and if made in advance, bring to room temperature before using for better blending of the ingredients. Shake well and toss onto salad.

GROCERY LIST	(QUANTITY)
FRESH	
Bean sprouts	½ cup
Garlic clove	1
Mushrooms	½ cup
Red onion	¼
Spinach	10 oz.
Baby spinach, prewashed	
CANS/JARS	
Canola oil	¼ cup
Ketchup	¼ cup
Soy sauce	dash
Red wine vinegar	¼ cup
Water chestnuts	4 oz. can
BAKING	
Sugar	1 T.
DAIRY	
Eggs	2
MEAT	
Bacon	¼ lb.

Grilled scallops with lime sauce

3 pounds large sea scallops

½ cup extra virgin olive oil

Kosher salt, pinch

Peppercorns, grind to personal preference

4 garlic cloves, minced

Combine above ingredients and chill for 30-60 minutes. Then skewer for easier cooking on grill, prepare sauce next.

2 limes zested

6 limes juiced

½ cup white wine, such as chardonnay or pinot grigio

2 T. fresh ginger, minced

2 shallots, finely chopped

2/3 cup cream

4 T. sweet chili sauce

12 T. butter

In a small saucepan, combine lime zest, juice, wine, ginger and shallot and cook until reduced in half. Add cream and reduce by half again, taking care to keep it at a simmer only. Turn heat off and add chili sauce and butter, mixing well. Keep warm.

Preheat grill to high heat, then spray with non-stick spray. Place skewers in a hinged, wire holder meant for grilling food so as to keep them from twisting around on the skewers while cooking. Grill scallops about 3-4 minutes per side, taking care not to overcook. Remove from skewers and divide amongst 8 plates, then top with lime sauce. Serves 8.

GROCERY LIST	(QUANTITY)
FRESH	
Garlic cloves	4
Limes	6
Ginger	2 T.
Shallots	2
CANS/JARS	
Olive oil	½ cup
Extra virgin	
Sweet chili sauce	4 T.
(May need to check in the ethnic section of the market, i.e. Asian)	
BAKING	
Kosher salt	pinch
Peppercorns	to taste
Non-stick spray	
DAIRY	
Cream	2/3 cup
Butter	12 T.
MEAT	
Sea scallops	3 lbs.
MISC.	
White wine	½ cup
Skewers	
Metal hinged food holder	
For grilling	

Phyllo-wrapped asparagus

**2 large bunches of asparagus,
washed, ends cut off**

1 16-ounce box of phyllo dough, defrosted

**1 cup butter,
melted in microwave-safe glass container**

2 cups fresh Parmesan cheese, grated

2 lemons, juiced

Unroll phyllo dough and remove one piece, spreading it flat and horizontally on a silicone mat or similar surface. Brush (using pastry brush) with butter, then fold in half horizontally, retaining the length, buttering again. Then take ~1/4 cup grated cheese and sprinkle it over dough. Next place 5 stalks of asparagus and place at one end of the phyllo dough, sprinkle with lemon juice. Start rolling up asparagus in dough until the end of the dough is reached, brushing butter on dough, making sure to butter and seal the end well. Place in a glass baking dish, sealed side down, and bake at 375 degrees until browned and dough is baked, about 15 minutes. Serve hot.

GROCERY LIST	(QUANTITY)
FRESH	
Asparagus	2
Large bunches	
Lemon	2
DAIRY	
Butter	1 cup
Parmesan cheese	2 cups
Fresh	
FROZEN	
Phyllo dough	1 box

Saffron wild rice pilaf

1 cup uncooked wild rice
1 onion, diced
8 T. butter
2 cups chicken stock
2 T. saffron
1 cup long grain rice, uncooked
Salt to taste, optional

Sauté onion in butter until limp. In a saucepan, bring chicken stock to a simmer with saffron added. Into a 2 ½ quart baking dish with cover (or foil), mix long grain rice and onion, mixing well. Add the chicken stock. Bake covered for 45 minutes at 350 degrees. While baking, prepare wild rice according to directions. Yield will be 2 cups. Add wild rice to long grain rice mixture, salt to taste, serve.

GROCERY LIST	(QUANTITY)
FRESH	
Onion 1	
Medium	
CANS/JARS	
Chicken stock . . . . . 2 cups	
DRY	
Long grain rice . . . . 1 cup	
Saffron . . . . 2 T.	
Salt . . . . to taste	
Wild rice . . . . 1 cup	
DAIRY	
Butter . . . . 8 T.	
(4 oz., 1 stick)	

Chocolate orange biscotti

2 1/8 cups flour
1 ½ tsp. baking powder
¼ tsp. salt
¾ cup sugar
8 T. butter, room temperature
2 eggs
2 T. orange liqueur (like Grand Marnier)
1 T. orange zest
1 cup pecans, toasted and chopped
6 ounces bittersweet chocolate, chopped
4 oz. semisweet chocolate for dipping, optional

Mix together flour, baking powder and salt, set aside. In another bowl, beat sugar and butter to blend. Beat in eggs, liqueur and zest. Add flour mixture and mix until blended. Stir in pecans and chocolate. Divide dough into halves, wrap in plastic wrap and place in freezer for 20 minutes.

Line large baking sheet with parchment paper. Heat oven to 350 degrees. With floured hands, form each dough half into a 16" log. Place each log on the parchment paper being careful that they do not touch each other. Bake 30 minutes until golden. Transfer parchment to cooling rack carefully and cool for 20 minutes. Reduce oven temperature to 300 degrees.

Next, place log on cutting board and cut, using serrated knife,

(Continued on next page)

GROCERY LIST	(QUANTITY)
FRESH	
Orange	1
For 1 T. zest	
BAKING	
Baking powder	1 ½ tsp.
Chocolate	6 oz.
Bittersweet	
Chocolate	4 oz.
Semisweet, optional	
Flour	2 1/8 cups
+ enough to use when handling dough	
Salt	¼ tsp.
Sugar	¾ cup
Pecans	1 cup
DAIRY	
Butter	8 T.
Eggs	2
MISC.	
Grand Marnier	2 T.
Or orange liqueur	
Parchment paper	1 box

into 1/2" slices. Stand slices upright on baking sheet (with the parchment paper) spaced apart. Repeat with 2nd log.

Bake biscotti until dry to touch and golden, about 30 minutes. Cool completely on rack. Optional step: melt 4 ounces semisweet chocolate in double boiler. Dip one end of biscotti into chocolate and let excess drip off. Place on wax paper to dry. Place biscotti in airtight containers and chill. Makes about 2 dozen.

Grocery list

FRESH

Asparagus 2
Large bunches

Bean sprouts. . . . . . ½ cup

Garlic clove 5

Ginger. . . . . 2 T.

Lemons 2

Limes 6

Mushrooms . . . . . ½ cup

Onion 1
Medium

Orange 1
For 1 T. zest

Red onion . . . . ¼

Shallot 2

Spinach . . . . 10 oz.
Baby spinach, prewashed

CANS/JARS

Artichoke bottoms 1
14 oz. can; in water

Canola oil . . . . ¼ cup

Chicken stock . . . . 2 cups

Olive oil. . . . . ½ cup
Extra virgin

Ketchup . . . . ¼ cup

Red wine vinegar . . ¼ cup

Soy sauce . . . . dash
+ enough to drizzle over all; optional

Sun dried tomatoes 1
Small jar

Sweet chili sauce . . . . 4 T.
(Check Asian section)

Water chestnuts 3
5 oz. cans, whole

DRY

Longrain rice . . . . . 1 cup
Uncooked

Wild rice . . . . 1 cup
Uncooked

FROZEN

Phyllo dough . . . . . 1 box

BAKING

Baking powder . . . 1½ tsp.

Chocolate . . . . 6 oz.
Bittersweet

Brown sugar . . . . . . ½ cup

Flour . . . . 2 1/8 cups
+ enough to use when
handling dough

Kosher salt . . . . . pinch x2

Non-stick spray

Parchment paper . . . 1 box

Pecans . . . . 1 cup

Peppercorns . . . . . to taste

Saffron . . . . 2 T.

Salt . . . . ¼ tsp.

Chocolate . . . . 4 oz.
Semisweet, optional

Sugar . . . . . ¾ cup + 1 T.

DAIRY

Basil pesto 1
6 oz. container

Butter. . . . . 2¾ cups + 6 T.

Cream . . . . 2/3 cup

Eggs 4

Mozzarella cheese 1
Fresh, 8 oz. container

Parmesan cheese . . 2 cups
Fresh

MEAT

Bacon . . . . 1¼ lb.
Uncooked, not microwave variety

Sea scallops . . . . . . 3 lbs.

MISC.

Grand Marnier . . . . . . 2 T.
Or orange liqueur

Metal hinged food holder
For grilling

Round toothpicks 1
Small box

Skewers

White wine . . . . . . ½ cup

Grilled shrimp k-bobs

MENU

Spanakopitas

Chicken salsa cups

Apple, walnut and blue cheese salad

Grilled shrimp k-bobs

Lemony beans and carrots

Spinach and goat cheese fettuccine

Cinnamon sugar apples

Spanakopitas

4 Tablespoons extra virgin olive oil

1 large onion, diced

2 cloves garlic, minced

2 10-ounce packages frozen chopped spinach, thawed and squeezed dry

¼ - ½ teaspoon ground pepper

½ teaspoon dried dill weed

¼ teaspoon nutmeg

Pinch salt

6 ounces feta cheese, crumbled

1 lemon, juiced

2 eggs

1 ¼ cups butter, melted

**16 ounces phyllo dough
(won't quite use the entire amount)**

In a large frying pan, sauté onion and garlic in olive oil until limp. Add spinach, stir. Remove from heat and add pepper, dill, nutmeg, salt, cheese, lemon juice and eggs. Mix well.

On a non-stick surface, unroll the phyllo dough keeping all but the one being used under the waxed paper wrap with a damp towel on top to prevent drying. With a pizza cutter, cut dough lengthwise into 2-3" strips. With a pastry brush, butter each strip. Then, in the lower corner, put a heaping teaspoon of spinach mixture onto each strip. Begin rolling up side to side forming triangles. Seal ends with butter. Place on large baking sheet. Repeat until all spinach has been used. Bake at 400 degrees 10 minutes, will be golden brown. Makes 64 spinach triangles.

GROCERY LIST	(QUANTITY)
FRESH	
Garlic cloves	2
Lemon	1
Onion	1
Large	
CANS/JARS	
Olive oil.	4 T.
Extra virgin	
BAKING	
Dill weed	½ tsp.
Nutmeg	¼ tsp.
Peppercorns	¼-½ tsp.
Salt	pinch
DAIRY	
Butter	1¼ cups
Eggs	2
Feta cheese	6 oz.
(Check deli)	
FROZEN	
Phyllo dough	16 oz.
Spinach	2
10 oz. bags	

Chicken salsa cups

24 Won ton wrappers (3" square)

1 pound chicken breasts, boned and skinned, or chicken tenders

1 ½ T. extra virgin olive oil

3/4 cup thick and chunky red salsa

1 tsp. cumin

¼ cup cilantro, chopped

¼ cup sharp cheddar cheese, shredded

¼ cup black olives, chopped

1 avocado, optional

Heat oven to 400 degrees. Place won ton wrappers in mini muffin tins after spraying the tins with non-stick cooking spray. Tuck wrappers in carefully until they conform to the shape of the cups with corners standing up. Bake for 6 minutes or until golden brown and crisp, place on a serving platter.

Meanwhile, dice chicken and brown in oil until cooked, then add salsa, cumin, cilantro, cheese and olives until heated thoroughly. Fill won ton cups with this mixture and serve. Garnish each cup with a small sliver of avocado, if desired.

GROCERY LIST	(QUANTITY)
FRESH	
Avocado	1
Optional	
Cilantro	1 bunch
Won ton wrappers	24
In refrigerator adjacent to produce section.	
CANS/JARS	
Black olives	¼ cup
Chopped	
Olive oil	1½ T.
Extra virgin	
Salsa	¾ cup
Red, chunky (hot if desired)	
BAKING	
Cumin	1 tsp.
DAIRY	
Cheddar cheese	¼ cup
Sharp	
MEAT	
Chicken breasts	1 lb.
Skinned and boned; or chicken tenders	

Apple, walnut and blue cheese salad

VINAIGRETTE

¼ cup extra virgin olive oil

¼ cup walnut oil

¼ cup balsamic vinegar

1 T. shallot, finely chopped

1 T. Dijon mustard

½ tsp. freshly ground pepper

¼ tsp. salt

1/8 tsp. each cinnamon, nutmeg and allspice

SALAD

1 10-ounce bag fresh spinach, prewashed

2 medium firm apples (such as Fuji, Granny Smith or Braeburn), thinly sliced. Sprinkle with lemon juice if cut in advance and put into a zip lock baggie to keep from turning brown.

¾ cup walnuts, chopped and toasted
(Toast in skillet on top of stove, directly in pan, no oil. Watch carefully!)

1 4-ounce container blue cheese, crumbled

Prepare vinaigrette by mixing all ingredients in a covered container. If made in advance, bring to room temperature before using. Whisk.

(Continued on next page)

GROCERY LIST	(QUANTITY)

FRESH

Apples 2
Firm ones, i.e. Fuji, Granny Smith or Braeburn

Lemon 1
(Enough juice to sprinkle on apples)

Shallot 1

Spinach 1
10-oz. bag

DAIRY

Blue cheese . . . . . . 4 oz.
Crumbled

CANS/JARS

Balsamic vinegar . . ¼ cup

Dijon mustard . . . . . . 1 T.

Olive oil . . . . ¼ cup
Extra virgin

Walnut oil . . . . . . ¼ cup

BAKING

Allspice . . . . 1/8 tsp.

Cinnamon . . . . . . 1/8 tsp.

Nutmeg . . . . 1/8 tsp.

Pepper . . . . ½ tsp.

Salt . . . . ¼ tsp.

Walnuts . . . . ¾ cup

In a large salad bowl, toss spinach greens with vinaigrette until coated lightly. Divide equally onto 8 salad plates. Arrange apple slices, toasted walnuts and blue cheese on top of spinach. Drizzle additional vinaigrette over tops and serve immediately.

Grilled shrimp k-bobs

3 pounds of raw, cleaned, deveined shrimp
Seasoned Salt
Paprika
Extra virgin olive oil
Wooden skewers
4 strips bacon, optional, cut into ½ inch pieces

Soak skewers in water for several hours before using to avoid burning on grill. Skewer shrimp (alternating with bacon if used) and set in plastic container with liquid-proof lid. (See photo so as to skewer them in such a way as to have them cook evenly and thoroughly.) Repeat until all shrimp have been used up. Drizzle olive oil over each shrimp, then sprinkle paprika and seasoned salt over all. For a little more of a kick in flavor, use paprika very generously, otherwise just sprinkle it on moderately. Flip plastic container a few times to evenly distribute seasonings and oil. Prepare grill on high and grill about 4-5 minutes per side. Serve immediately. Serves 8.

GROCERY LIST	(QUANTITY)

CANS/JARS
Olive oil. . . . . ½ cup
Extra virgin

BAKING
Paprika . . . small container
Salt . . . . . . small container
Seasoned

MEAT
Shrimp. . . . . .3 lbs.
Fresh or frozen, deveined, raw
Bacon . . . . 4 strips
Optional

MISC.
Wooden skewers

Lemony beans and carrots

1 pound green beans, trimmed
1 pound baby carrots, cut julienne-style
2 T. butter, melted
Juice of one lemon
Zest of one lemon
½ tsp. turmeric

Steam vegetables in either the microwave or in a vegetable steamer until al dente. While vegetables are cooking, in a small saucepan melt butter and add in lemon juice, zest and turmeric. Toss over cooked vegetables and serve hot.

GROCERY LIST	(QUANTITY)
FRESH	
Baby carrots	1 lb.
Green beans	1 lb.
Lemon	1
BAKING	
Turmeric	½ tsp.
DAIRY	
Butter	2 T.

Spinach and goat cheese fettuccine

1 pound spinach fettuccine, dried

10 ounces baby spinach, washed and chopped

2/3 cup chicken broth, low sodium

1 pound goat cheese, broken into chunks

2 cups cherry tomatoes, washed and cut in half, room temperature

Pepper to taste

Boil water in large pot and cook pasta until al dente, then add spinach to water and boil until wilted, about a minute. Drain and then return to pot, cover.

In a larger saucepan, boil chicken broth. Stir in goat cheese and melt. Remove from heat. Add cheese mixture to pasta, mix, toss in tomatoes, grind pepper over all. Serves 8.

GROCERY LIST	(QUANTITY)
FRESH	
Baby spinach	10 oz.
Cherry tomatoes	2 cups
CANS/JARS	
Chicken broth	2/3 cup
BAKING	
Peppercorns	to taste
DRY	
Spinach fettuccine	1 lb.
DAIRY	
Goat cheese	1 lb.

Cinnamon sugar apples

8 small Granny Smith apples, washed, peeled and cored (reserve some of the peels)

8 ounces cream cheese, softened

1 tsp. cinnamon

1 T. sugar

2 T. butter

2 ounces walnuts, chopped

Caramel sauce

1 box puff pastry, defrosted in refrigerator

Combine cream cheese, cinnamon, sugar, butter and walnuts thoroughly. With reserved peels, push to bottom of apples to close hole in bottom created by coring. Then fill each apple with cream cheese mixture. Spread out both sheets of puff pasty and roll a bit thinner with rolling pin. Cut each sheet into 6-squares (there will be 4 extra ones) and place an apple in the center of each one. Pull the 4 corners up to the top of the apple, then pinch the sides together. Place on a baking sheet, brush with milk and bake for 40 minutes at 350 degrees. Serve with cinnamon or vanilla ice cream. Serves 8.

GROCERY LIST	(QUANTITY)
FRESH	
Apples	8
Granny Smith, small	
BAKING	
Cinnamon	1 tsp.
Sugar	1 T.
Walnuts	2 oz.
DAIRY	
Butter	2 T.
Cream cheese	8 oz.
FROZEN	
Caramel sauce	
Puff pastry	1 box

Grocery list

FRESH

Apples. 10
2 firm ones: Fuji, or Braeburn
+ 8 small Granny Smith

Avocado 1
Optional

Baby carrots. . . . . . 1 lb.
Peeled

Baby spinach . . . . .10 oz.

Cherry tomatoes . . .2 cups

Cilantro . . . . .1 bunch

Garlic cloves 2

Green beans . . . . . . 1 lb.

Lemons 3

Onion . . . . 1 large

Shallot. 1

Spinach 1
10 oz. bag

Won ton wrappers . . . 24
In refrigerator adjacent
to produce section

CANS/JARS

Balsamic vinegar . . .¼ cup

Black olives . . . . . . ¼ cup
Chopped

Chicken broth. . . .2/3 cup
Low sodium

Dijon mustard. . . . . . .1 T.

Olive oil . . . 1 cup + 1½ T.
Extra virgin

Salsa. . . . . ¾ cup
Red, chunky (hot if desired)

Walnut oil . . . . ¼ cup

DRY

Spinach fettuccine. . . 1 lb.

BAKING

Allspice . . . . .1/8 tsp.

Cinnamon . . . 1 1/8 tsp.

Cumin . . . . .1 tsp.

Dill weed . . . . ½ tsp.

Nutmeg. . .¼ tsp. + 1/8 tsp.

Paprika . . .small container

Peppercorns. . .1 T. + ½ tsp.

Salt . . . . .¼ + tsp.

Seasoned Salt. 1
Small container

Sugar . . . . 1 T.

Turmeric. . . . . ½ tsp.

Walnuts. . . . ¾ cup + 2 oz.

DAIRY

Blue cheese 1
4 oz.container; crumbled

Butter. . . . . 1½ cups

Cream cheese . . . . .8 oz.

Eggs 2

Feta cheese . . . . . .6 oz.
(Check deli)

Goat cheese. . . . . . 1 lb.

Cheddar cheese . . . ¼ cup
Sharp

MEAT

Chicken breasts . . . . 1 lb.
Skinned and boned,
or chicken tenders

Shrimp. . . . . .3 lbs.
Fresh or frozen, deveined, raw

Bacon . . . . 4 strips
Optional

FROZEN

Caramel sauce
Near ice cream

Phyllo dough . . . . .16 oz.

Puff pastry . . . . . . 1 box

Spinach. 2
10 oz. bags

MISC.

Wooden skewers

Herb-crusted pork tenderloin with red currant sauce

MENU

Pesto-stuffed cherry tomatoes

Olive tapanade tapas

Broccoli salad

Herb-crusted pork tenderloin
with red currant sauce

Snap peas, tomatoes and basil

Twice-baked pesto potatoes

Apple crisp

Pesto-stuffed cherry tomatoes FRONT COVER PHOTO

Cherry tomatoes – 1 container, washed
Pesto – prepared, basil
Fresh mozzarella cheese, sliced into thin slices
Fresh basil for garnish
Balsamic vinegar

Slice tops off tomatoes about ¾ of the way up. Scoop out insides and discard (or save for another use along with the tops), then turn "shells" upside down on paper toweling to drain. Fill shells with pesto, then push a slice of cheese down along the side of the pesto/tomato. Place in ovenproof dish and heat until warm, about ten minutes at 325 degrees. Place on decorative serving dish, garnish with a leaf of basil tucked into the pesto. Drizzle balsamic vinegar over tops of tomatoes, allowing it to drip down onto serving dish as a decorative touch.

I love having a basil plant in my kitchen so that the leaves are readily available for recipes like this. I purchased mine at a natural food, farmers' market type of grocery store and was ten dollars well spent!

GROCERY LIST	(QUANTITY)
FRESH	
Cherry tomatoes . . 1 container	
(Do not buy grape tomatoes as they will tip over when filled!)	
Basil . . . . 1 package	
Or buy the entire plant	
CANS/JARS	
Balsamic vinegar	
Enough for drizzling	
DAIRY	
Pesto . . . . 1 container	
Basil type	
Mozzarella cheese	
Fresh type in liquid	

Delicious
10/9/12

Olive tapanade tapas

4 oz. Black olives, pitted
1 clove garlic
3 T. Pine nuts, toasted
3 T. Extra virgin olive oil
4 oz. Blue cheese, crumbled
French Bread or Baguette

Slice bread into 1/2" pieces and brush both sides with 2 T. olive oil and season with salt and pepper. Place on cookie sheet.

Toast in a 350 degree oven until golden brown, about 5 minutes.

Mix in a food processor: garlic, pine nuts and olives until coarsely chopped. Add 1 T. oil in a thin stream until combined.

Place olive mixture in a bowl. Add crumbled blue cheese and mix gently, being careful not to over mix and break the cheese up too much.

Spread on toast and garnish with pine nuts.

GROCERY LIST	(QUANTITY)
FRESH	
Garlic	1 clove
Pine nuts	3 T.
CANS/JARS	
Black olives	1
4 oz. can; pitted	
Olive oil.	3 T.
Extra virgin	
DRY	
French bread or baguette	
DAIRY	
Blue cheese	4 oz.
Crumbled	

Broccoli salad

1 bunch fresh broccoli
½ pound bacon or bacon bit equivalent
½ medium red onion, chopped
½ cup raisins
1 cup whole cashews or almonds
1 cup light mayonnaise
1/8 cup sugar
4 tsp. red wine vinegar

Make dressing using the mayonnaise, sugar and vinegar, stirring, letting sit long enough for sugar to dissolve.

Cut washed broccoli into bite-sized pieces, using stems and flowers. Submerge for one minute into boiling water to "take the raw out" and then rinse with cold water until cold, drain. Cut bacon into small pieces and fry until crisp. Drain. Combine broccoli, bacon, onion, raisins and nuts in a salad bowl. Toss dressing on salad. Serve on individual plates.

GROCERY LIST (QUANTITY)

FRESH
Broccoli . . . . 1 lb.
Red onion . . . . ½

CANS/JARS
Mayonnaise . . . . . . 1 cup
Light
Red wine vinegar . . .4 tsp.

BAKING
Raisins . . . . ½ cup
Cashews, whole . . . 1 cup
(Or almonds)
Sugar . . . . .1/8 cup

MEAT
Bacon . . . . .½ lb.
(Regular, microwave or bacon bit equivalent)

Herb-crusted pork tenderloin with red currant sauce

1 1-1 ¼ lb. pork tenderloin
1 T. Dijon or yellow mustard
Salt and pepper
1 T. fresh rosemary, minced
2 tsp. fresh thyme, minced
2 tsp. fresh sage, minced
2 T. olive oil
1/3 cup red currant jelly
1 T. white wine vinegar
2 tsp. butter, softened
1 tsp. horseradish
¼ tsp. lemon zest
1 lemon, juiced

1. Trim any fat from pork. Brush meat evenly with mustard. Sprinkle meat with salt and black pepper. In a shallow dish, combine rosemary, thyme and sage. Roll meat in the mixed herbs, pressing herbs onto all sides of the meat.

2. In a very large, nonstick skillet, brown the meat in hot oil over medium-high heat, turning to brown all sides. Transfer to a rack in a shallow roasting pan.

(Continued on next page)

GROCERY LIST	(QUANTITY)
FRESH	
Fresh rosemary	1 T.
Fresh thyme	2 tsp.
Fresh sage	2 tsp.
Lemon	1
BAKING	
Salt and pepper to taste	
CANS/JARS	
Mustard	1 T.
Dijon or yellow	
Olive oil	2 T.
Extra virgin	
Red currant jelly	1/3 cup
White wine vinegar	1 T.
Horseradish	1 tsp.
(Regular, non-creamy)	
DAIRY	
Butter	2 tsp.
MEAT	
Pork tenderloin	1-1¼ lb.

Roast in a 425 degree oven about 25 minutes or until thermometer says 155 degrees and juices run clear. Remove from the oven and cover with foil 15 minutes. Thermometer will rise to 160.

3. Currant Sauce – In a small saucepan, stir together the jelly, vinegar and butter. Heat and stir until jelly is melted. Remove from heat. Stir in horseradish, lemon peel and lemon juice.

4. To serve, slice pork and arrange on serving platter, spooning sauce over. Serve remaining sauce on side.

Snap peas, tomatoes and basil

3 T. extra virgin olive oil

1 cup white onion, finely chopped

2 garlic cloves, minced

1 ½ pounds snap peas, ends trimmed

4 Roma tomatoes, chopped

**1 cup fresh basil leaves,
cut up using kitchen shears**

Heat oil in large ~14″ skillet over medium heat. Add onion and garlic and sauté until onion wilts, about five minutes. Add snap peas, tomatoes and basil leaves, stirring and heating thoroughly. Cover and turn heat off. Season to taste with salt and pepper, keeping covered until ready to serve.

GROCERY LIST	(QUANTITY)
FRESH	
White onion	1
Garlic cloves	2
Snap peas	1 ½ lbs.
Tomatoes	4
Any kind	
Basil leaves	1 cup
CANS/JARS	
Olive oil.	3 T.
Extra virgin	

Twice-baked pesto potatoes

8 Baking potatoes, baked
1 cup fresh basil
¼ cup prepared pesto
¼ cup plain yogurt
¼ cup half and half
¾ cup fresh Parmesan cheese, grated
(or Pecorino Romano)
2 T. butter
1 tsp. garlic powder
Salt and pepper to taste
Paprika for garnish

Steam basil leaves over boiling water for 1 minute, set aside to cool and then chop in a food processor. Place potatoes on a flat side and slice off the "top" horizontally, about 4/5ths of the way up from the bottom. Set tops aside. Gently scoop out potatoes leaving 1/8" around the edges and bottom, putting scooped potatoes in a bowl. (Use a small knife to first create an even edge and then use a melon baller to scoop the potato out.) In a small saucepan, heat the pesto, yogurt, cheese and butter. Add basil, pesto, yogurt, half and half and cheese to bowl of potatoes along with garlic powder. Using a hand mixer, whip up until well blended and fairly smooth. Add salt and pepper to taste.

Then fill the cavities of the scooped-out potatoes until slightly

(Continued on next page)

GROCERY LIST	(QUANTITY)
FRESH	
Baking potatoes	8
Basil	1 cup
BAKING	
Garlic powder	1 tsp.
Paprika For garnish, sprinkling	
Salt and pepper	to taste
DAIRY	
Basil pesto	¼ cup
Butter	2 T.
Half and half	¼ cup
Parmesan cheese Fresh; or Pecorino Romano	¾ cup
Plain yogurt	¼ cup

mounded up higher than the top edge. Place filled potatoes in a sprayed, glass baking dish, sprinkle with paprika, bake at 350 degrees for 20-30 minutes (until hot.)

Most likely there will be more filling than the potatoes will hold. Therefore, save it in an airtight container to serve another day as "mashed potatoes."

Use the extra potato tops as a snack – sprinkle with seasoned salt and warm in microwave.

Apple crisp

3 cups apples, peeled and sliced

Butter

2/3 cups brown sugar + extra for sprinkling

½ cup flour

2 cups old fashioned oatmeal

½ cup butter, melted

½ tsp. each cinnamon, nutmeg and cloves

¼ cup walnuts, chopped

Vanilla ice cream

Butter bottom and sides of an 8 inch square, glass cooking dish. Spread apples evenly across the bottom. Sprinkle very lightly with brown sugar and dot with butter.

Mix together the 2/3 cups brown sugar, oats, melted butter, spices and nuts. Sprinkle the topping over the apples and bake in a 350 degree oven for 45 minutes. Topping will be nice and crispy. Excellent served warm with vanilla ice cream.

GROCERY LIST	(QUANTITY)
FRESH	
Apples	3 cups
Various hard, tart ones, sliced	
DRY	
Oats	2 cups
Old fashioned	
BAKING	
Brown sugar	2/3+ cups
Flour	½ cup
Cinnamon, nutmeg and cloves	½ tsp. each
Walnuts	¼ cup
Chopped	
DAIRY	
Butter	½ cup +
FROZEN	
Vanilla ice cream	
With vanilla beans	

Grocery list HERB-CRUSTED PORK TENDERLOIN MENU

FRESH

Apples. . . . . .3 cups
Various hard, tart ones, sliced

Baking potatoes 8

Basil . . .2 cups + 1 package
Or buy the entire plant.

Broccoli . . . . 1 lb.

Cherry tomatoes . . 1 container
(Do not buy grape tomatoes as they will tip over when filled!)

Fresh rosemary . . . . . . 1 T.

Fresh sage . . . . .2 tsp.

Fresh thyme . . . . . . .2 tsp.

Garlic cloves 3

Lemon 1

Pine nuts . . . . 2 T.

Red onion . . . . ½

Snap peas . . . . . . 1 ½ lbs.

Tomatoes 4
Any kind

White onion 1

CANS/JARS

Balsamic vinegar
Enough for drizzling

Black olives . . . .4 oz. can
Pitted

Mustard . . . . 1 T.
Dijon or yellow

Olive oil . . . . ½ cup
Extra virgin

Horseradish . . . . . . .1 tsp.
(Regular, non-creamy)

Mayonnaise . . . . . . 1 cup

Red currant jelly . .1/3 cup

Red wine vinegar . . .4 tsp.

White wine vinegar. . . 1 T.

DRY

French bread or baguette . . 1

Oats . . . . .2 cups
Old fashioned

BAKING

Brown sugar. . . 2/3+ cups

Cashews *Whole* . . . . 1 cup

Cinnamon, nutmeg
and cloves . . . ½ tsp. each

Flour . . . . ½ cup

Garlic powder . . . . .1 tsp.

Paprika
For garnish, sprinkling

Raisins . . . . ½ cup

Salt and pepper . . to taste

Sugar . . . . .1/8 cup

Walnuts . . . . ¼ cup
Chopped

DAIRY

Blue cheese . . . . . . .4 oz.
Crumbled

Butter . . . . >½ cup
+2 T. & 2 tsp.

Half and half . . . . . ¼ cup

Mozzarella cheese
Fresh type, in liquid

Parmesan cheese . . .¾ cup
(Fresh, or Pecorino Romano)

Pesto (basil type) 1
4-oz. container & ½ cup

Plain yogurt . . . . . . ¼ cup

MEAT

Bacon . . . . ½ lb.
(Regular, microwave or bacon bit equivalent)

Pork tenderloin . . . 1-1 ¼ lb.

FROZEN

Vanilla ice cream
With vanilla beans

Mushroom-crusted grilled steaks with blue cheese topping

MENU

Brie quesadillas with peach salsa

Spinach and orange salad
with poppy seed dressing

Mushroom-crusted grilled steaks
with blue cheese topping

Grilled zucchini

Spinach and cheese stuffed onions

Wild rice and mushrooms

Best basic cheesecake with
cherry topping

Brie quesadillas with peach salsa

1 package 8" tortillas
1 lb. brie, sliced thinly
Bunch of cilantro
1 cup mapled walnuts (see recipe below)
Butter

MAPLED WALNUTS:

1 cup coarsely chopped walnuts
2 T. maple syrup

Preheat oven to 300 degrees. Mix nuts and syrup, coating nuts completely. Spread them out onto a jellyroll pan and bake for 20 minutes, turning halfway through. Set aside to chill.

To assemble tortillas, place a few strips of brie on half a tortilla, a few nuts and cilantro sprigs. Press together firmly and set aside until all have been assembled. Then heat a very large frying pan with butter, taking care not to burn the butter. Place 2 quesadillas inside pan to cook at a time, cooking just long enough to brown each side and to melt the cheese. Place on a baking sheet in warm oven while all are being cooked. To serve, cut each tortilla into 3 triangles using a pizza cutter (if available) and serve with peach salsa.

(Continued on next page)

GROCERY LIST	(QUANTITY)
FRESH	
Cilantro	1 bunch
CANS/JARS	
Maple syrup	2 T.
DRY	
Tortillas, 8"	1 package
Walnuts	1 cup
DAIRY	
Brie	1 lb. wheel
Butter	1 stick
FRESH	
Pepper Serrano or jalapeno	1
Scallions	3
Red bell pepper	½
Cilantro	½ cup
Lime	1
CANS/JARS	
Peaches	29 oz. can
Lite, in pear juice	
Olive oil Extra virgin	2 T.
BAKING/DRY	
Cumin	1 tsp.
Pepper	½ tsp.
Salt	¼ tsp.
Tortilla chips	
Or quesadillas above	

PEACH SALSA

1 29-oz. can lite peaches in pear juice, drained and chopped

½ Serrano or jalapeno pepper, seeded and chopped

3 scallions, chopped

½ red bell pepper, chopped

½ cup cilantro, chopped

1 lime, juiced

1 tsp. cumin

½ tsp. ground pepper

2 T. extra virgin olive oil

¼ tsp. salt

Mix all and serve with favorite tortilla chips or use with above quesadillas.

Spinach and orange salad with poppy seed dressing

10 oz. fresh baby spinach, prewashed

1 11-oz. can mandarin oranges, drained

½ small red onion, sliced thinly

2 T. sunflower nuts, toasted

POPPY SEED DRESSING:

¾ cup sugar

1 tsp. dry mustard

1 tsp. salt

1/3 cup raspberry vinegar

1 T. onion, grated

1 cup extra virgin olive oil

1 ½ tsp. poppy seeds

Place spinach in large bowl and add orange pieces, onion and sunflower nuts. Toss to combine. Cover and chill until ready to serve, preparing dressing next. Before serving, toss salad with desired amount of dressing, serve. Makes 6-8 servings.

DRESSING:

Place sugar, dry mustard, salt, vinegar and onion in a food processor and process until combined. While still running, add olive oil through top in slow, steady stream. Then add the poppy seeds, pulsating until mixed. Will make 1½ cups.

GROCERY LIST	(QUANTITY)
FRESH	
Baby spinach	1
10 oz. bag	
Red onion	½
Small	
Onion	1 T.
Grated	
CANS/JARS	
Mandarin oranges	1
11 oz. can	
Olive oil	1 cup
Extra virgin	
Raspberry vinegar	1/3 cup
DRY	
Sunflower nuts	2 T.
BAKING	
Dry mustard	1 tsp.
Poppy seeds	1½ tsp.
Salt	1 tsp.
Sugar	¾ cup

Mushroom-crusted grilled steaks with blue cheese topping

½ ounce package dried shitake or porcini mushrooms, minced in food processor

Freshly ground pepper, as preferred

6 ribeye steaks (or steaks of choice)

6 ounces blue cheese, crumbled

4 ounces cream cheese, softened

1 garlic clove, minced

1 shallot, chopped finely

1 T. fresh rosemary, minced

¼ cup toasted and chopped walnuts

Place mushroom crumbs and pepper in a flat dish. Dredge each steak through the mixture, coating both sides. Refrigerate until ready to grill. Next, prepare the topping by combining the blue cheese, cream cheese, garlic, shallot, rosemary and walnuts. Set aside, keeping at room temperature until ready to use, unless it is made the day before. Prepare grill and grill steaks as preferred on the first side. After flipping them, place a dollop of the topping on each steak and complete the grilling on side #2. The topping will melt a bit and spread out on top of the meat. Serve immediately. 6 steaks

GROCERY LIST	(QUANTITY)
FRESH	
Garlic clove	1
Shallot	1
Rosemary	1 T.
Shitake or porcini mushrooms	½ oz. package
Dried; (check Asian section)	
BAKING	
Peppercorns	
Walnuts	¼ cup
DAIRY	
Blue cheese	6 oz.
Cream cheese	4 oz.
MEAT	
Ribeye steaks	6
(or steaks of choice)	

Grilled zucchini

6 medium zucchini
Extra virgin olive oil
Kosher salt
Lemon pepper
Garlic powder

Wash and dry zucchini. Slice off both ends, then slice lengthwise into thin pieces, about 3/8" thick. Place on jellyroll pan without overlapping. Brush with olive oil, then sprinkle with lemon pepper, salt and garlic powder. Turn zucchini over and repeat. Heat grill and place vegetables on sprayed grate, grilling 2-3 minutes per side until cooked but not mushy. Serve each person the equivalent of ~one zucchini, less if they are very large. Serves 6-8.

GROCERY LIST	(QUANTITY)
FRESH	
Zucchini	6
Medium	
CANS/JARS	
Olive oil	~¼ cup
Extra virgin, enough to brush onto vegetable	
Cooking spray	
To spray grill grate	
BAKING	
Kosher salt	to sprinkle
Lemon pepper . .	to sprinkle
Garlic powder .	to sprinkle

Spinach and cheese stuffed onions

6 medium onions

Salt and water

1 10-ounce package frozen spinach, defrosted and drained thoroughly

4 ounces cream cheese, room temperature

½ + ¼ cup Parmesan cheese, grated

Pepper

Nutmeg

Paprika

Slice off both ends of onions to achieve a flat surface, then peel onions and place in large saucepan with one inch of salted water. Cover and bring to a boil, reduce heat and simmer for ten minutes or until onions are tender. Drain. Slice off the top of the onion about 4/5 of the way up. Scoop out the center leaving a ½" shell. Take a piece of the scooped out onion and place inside shell to close hole in bottom. Chop up the onion tops and combine with spinach, cream cheese, ½ cup Parmesan cheese, pepper and nutmeg to taste. Store scooped out onion pieces for later use. Lightly salt the empty onion shells, then fill with spinach mixture. Divide remaining ¼ cup cheese and sprinkle on top of each onion. Sprinkle with paprika. Bake at 350 degrees for 20-30 minutes until bubbly. Serves 6.

GROCERY LIST	(QUANTITY)
FRESH	
Onions	6
Medium	
BAKING	
Salt	
Peppercorns	
Nutmeg	
Paprika	
DAIRY	
Cream cheese	4 oz.
Parmesan cheese	¾ cup
FROZEN	
Spinach	10 oz.

There may be more spinach mixture than onions will hold, so use the leftovers for another meal over pasta or as the vegetable dish.

Wild rice and mushrooms

2/3 cup washed and sliced mushrooms
2 T. butter
1 medium onion, finely chopped
2 cups beef broth
½ cup wild rice, rinsed
1 cup long grain rice
2 T. snipped parsley

In a medium saucepan, sauté mushrooms and onion in butter until limp. Add broth and bring to boil. Add wild rice; reduce heat, cover and simmer for 20 minutes. Then add long grain rice, boil again, reduce heat and cover, simmering another 20 minutes longer or until the rice is all cooked. Add parsley, serve. Serves 6-8.

GROCERY LIST	(QUANTITY)
FRESH	
Mushrooms	2/3 cup
Onion	1
Medium	
Parsley	2 T.
CANS/JARS	
Beef broth	2 cups
DRY	
Long grain rice	1 cup
Wild rice	½ cup
DAIRY	
Butter	2 T.

Best basic cheesecake with cherry topping

CRUST:

8 graham crackers
crumbled in blender or food processor
½ cup walnuts
chopped finely or added to food processor
1/3 cup butter, melted
¼ cup sugar

Mix crust ingredients well until blended. Press into bottom and then sides of 9" springform pan that has been sprayed with cooking spray and has had sugar sprinkled inside it and shaken to reach both sides and bottom of pan. Set aside while preparing filling.

CHEESECAKE FILLING:

3 8-ounce packages cream cheese,
room temperature
1 ½ cups sugar
6 eggs, room temperature
2 cups sour cream, room temperature
2 T. cornstarch
1 T. lemon juice
2 tsp. vanilla

In a large mixing bowl, place cream cheese and beat with electric mixer until smooth. Slowly add sugar until blended. Next, slowly add eggs one at a time, then add sour cream, cornstarch, lemon juice and vanilla until blended. Pour into prepared crust and bake at 350 degrees for one hour.

(Continued on next page)

GROCERY LIST	(QUANTITY)
FRESH	
Lemons	2
DAIRY	
Butter.	1/3 cup
Cream cheese	3
8-oz. packages	
Eggs	6
Sour cream	2 cups
BAKING	
Cherry pie filling.	1
21 oz. can	
Cornstarch	2 T.
Graham crackers	8
Sugar	1¾ cups
Vanilla extract.	2 tsp.
Walnuts	½ cup

Turn off oven while leaving cake inside for another 30 minutes. Cool on cooling rack, then cover and chill. Unmold when ready to serve. Serve cherry topping over individual slices.

CHERRY TOPPING:

21 ounce can cherry pie filling

1 lemon, zest plus juice

Mix above ingredients and chill until ready to use.

Grocery list  MUSHROOM-CRUSTED GRILLED STEAKS MENU

FRESH

Baby spinach 1
10 oz. bag

Cilantro . . . 1 bunch + ½ cup

Mushrooms . . ½ oz. package
Dried shitake or porcini, check
Asian section

Garlic clove 1

Lemons 2

Lime 1

Mushrooms . . . . .2/3 cup

Onions 7
Medium + 1 T. grated

Parsley. . . . . .2 T.

Red bell pepper . . . . . ½

Red onion . . . . ½
Small

Rosemary. . . . . .1 T.

Scallions 3

Pepper
Serrano or jalapeno

Shallot. 1

Zucchini. 6
Medium

CANS/JARS

Beef broth . . . . . . .2 cups

Olive oil. . . . . . . 1½ cups
Extra virgin

Mandarin oranges. . 11 oz. can

Maple syrup. . . . . . . .2 T.

Peaches . . . . . .29 oz. can
Lite, in pear juice

Raspberry vinegar . . 1/3 cup

DRY

Long grain rice . . . . . 1 cup

Tortilla chips of choice
(If not making quesadillas)

Tortillas, 8". . . . 1 package

Wild rice . . . . ½ cup

BAKING

Cherry pie filling . . .21 oz. can

Cooking spray
To spray grill grate

Cornstarch . . . . 2 T.

Cumin . . . . .1 tsp.

Dry mustard . . . . . . .1 tsp.

Garlic powder . . .to sprinkle

Graham crackers 8

Kosher salt . . . . to sprinkle

Lemon pepper. . to sprinkle

Nutmeg

Paprika

Pepper. . . . . .½ + tsp.

Poppy seeds. . . . . 1½ tsp.

Salt . . . . .1¼ + tsp.

Sugar . . . . 2½ cups

Sunflower nuts . . . . . .2 T.

Vanilla extract. . . . .2 tsp.

Walnuts . . . . .2 cups

DAIRY

Blue cheese . . . . . . .6 oz.

Brie . . . . .1 lb. wheel

Butter. . . . . ~2 sticks

Cream cheese 4
8 oz. packages

Eggs 6

Parmesan cheese . . . ¾ cup
Fresh

Sour cream . . . . . .2 cups

MEAT

Ribeye steaks 6
(or steaks of choice)

FROZEN

Spinach. . . . . . . .10 oz.

Phyllo-wrapped salmon with pesto & cheese

MENU

Shrimp tortilla chip appetizer

Olive tapanade spirals

Spinach salad with hot bacon dressing

Phyllo-wrapped salmon with pesto and cheese

Artichoke and mushroom medley

Asparagus and pasta stir fry

Chocolate mousse

Shrimp tortilla chip appetizer

1 lb. uncooked shrimp, peeled and deveined
4 T. extra virgin olive oil
Salt and freshly ground pepper
2 avocadoes, ripe, chopped finely
¼ cup red onion, diced
½ jalapeno, diced
¼ cup lime juice, fresh
¼ cup cilantro, chopped
¼ cup tortilla chips, crushed
~25 tortilla chips, flat and round

Grill shrimp on hot grill after tossing in 2 T. of the olive oil and seasoned with salt and pepper. Grill for about a minute on each side to cook through. Place shrimp on cutting board and chop up very small. In a medium bowl, combine shrimp, 2 T. olive oil, avocados, onion, jalapeno, lime juice, cilantro and crushed tortilla chips, seasoning with salt and pepper to taste. Just before ready to serve to prevent soft and mushy tortilla chips, scoop heaping teaspoon of mixture onto a chip, serve on plate immediately.

GROCERY LIST	(QUANTITY)
FRESH	
Avocados	2
Red onion	1
Small	
Jalapeno pepper	½
Limes	4
Medium	
Cilantro	1 bunch
CANS/JARS	
Olive oil	4 T.
Extra virgin	
DRY	
Tortilla chips	13 oz. bag
Flat, round ones	
Salt	
Peppercorns for grinder	
FROZEN	
Shrimp	1 lb.
Uncooked, peeled and deveined preferable	

Olive tapanade spirals

11 ounces pitted Kalamata olives

1 T. crushed garlic

¼ cup toasted pine nuts

1 cup crumbled blue cheese

1 T. extra virgin olive oil

1 package Puff Pastry, defrosted in refrigerator

Mix olives, garlic, pine nuts, cheese and olive oil coarsely in food processor. Unwrap both sheets of puff pastry and flatten with rolling pin a bit. Spread olive tapanade over rectangle evenly. Starting with wider side of pastry, start to tightly roll until you have rolled it up. Wrap in plastic wrap and freeze for later use or chill to use sooner. When ready to use, cut into ~1/4" spirals and lay flat on jellyroll pan. Bake at 400 degrees for 20 minutes, serve hot.

GROCERY LIST	(QUANTITY)
FRESH	
Garlic	1 T.
Pine nuts	¼ cup
CANS/JARS	
Kalamata olives . . .	11 oz.
(Greek), pitted	
Olive oil.	1 T.
Extra virgin	
DAIRY	
Blue cheese	1 cup
Crumbled	
FROZEN	
Puff Pastry sheets . .	17.3 oz.

Spinach salad with hot bacon dressing

1 large egg
6 oz. fresh spinach, prewashed
3 T. red wine vinegar
½ tsp. sugar
¼ tsp. freshly ground pepper
Pinch Kosher salt
10 slices bacon, cut into ½" pieces
½ cup red onion, chopped,
1 garlic clove, minced

Place egg in small saucepan and cover with 1" water, bringing to a boil. Remove pan from heat, cover and let stand 10 minutes. Fill small bowl with ice water and transfer egg, standing 5 minutes, then peel, quarter and set aside. Don't leave in either hot or cold water too long or shell won't come off easily.

Place spinach in large salad bowl. Into a small bowl, mix vinegar, sugar, pepper and salt together, sitting long enough for sugar to dissolve.

(Continued on next page)

GROCERY LIST	(QUANTITY)
FRESH	
Spinach	6 oz.
Red onion	½ cup
Garlic clove	1
CANS/JARS	
Red wine vinegar	3 T.
DRY	
Sugar	½ tsp.
Pepper	¼ tsp.
Salt	pinch
Kosher	
DAIRY	
Egg	1 large
MEAT	
Bacon	10 slices
Do not buy microwave bacon as the fat is needed	

Cook bacon in frying pan until crisp, then drain on paper towels, reserving bacon drippings. Pour bacon fat into heatproof bowl, then return 3 T. of it to the frying pan. Add onion and garlic, cooking until soft. Then add vinegar mixture to pan, stirring while removing from heat. Scrape brown bits from bottom of pan to loosen. Pour hot dressing over the spinach, add the bacon and toss until spinach is wilted. Serve on individual plates, arrange egg on top and serve.

Phyllo-wrapped salmon with pesto & cheese

1 package phyllo dough
Will need 12-12"x17" pieces, thawed
(may need to piece together to make them this
size if only the narrower ones are available)
4 ounces butter, melted
1 ½ pound wild salmon fillet, skinned
(slightly more would be fine)
8 ounces cream cheese, room temperature
1 lemon, zested
1 T. capers
1/3 cup prepared pesto
¼ cup sun dried tomatoes, chopped

Place a sheet of parchment paper the size of the phyllo dough on a jellyroll pan, then begin with the layers of phyllo, placing them on top of each other, brushing butter between the layers. Place the salmon lengthwise down the center of the dough, leaving about an inch at the top (narrower end) and trimming the bottom end to within an inch also. Grind fresh peppercorns over fish. In a small bowl, mix the cream cheese, zest and capers thoroughly. Spread the cream cheese evenly over the salmon, then spread the pesto over the cheese, then sprinkle the tomato pieces over the pesto.

Fold one side of dough over the fish, butter the dough, then

(Continued on next page)

GROCERY LIST	(QUANTITY)
FRESH	
Lemon 1	
CANS/JARS	
Sun dried tomatoes. . ¼ cup	
Capers . . . . 1 T.	
BAKING	
Peppercorns	
DAIRY	
Butter. . . . . .4 oz.	
Cream cheese . . . . .8 oz.	
Pesto Prepared . . . . .1/3 cup	
MEAT	
Salmon, wild . . . . 1½ lbs.	
Or slightly more	
FROZEN	
Phyllo dough . . 1 package	
(Or "filo," should be near the frozen pie crusts)	

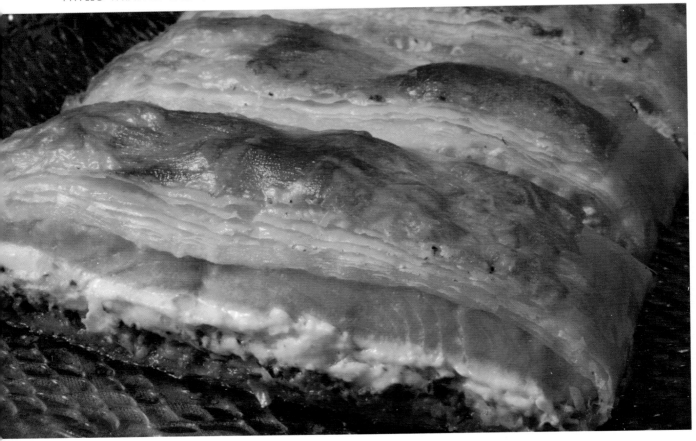

fold the other side over the first and seal. Seal the one inch
ends together and use butter or water to do so, if necessary.
Never allow the dough to dry out or it will crack. Flip the
bundle over so that the seams are underneath. With a sharp
knife, cut 6 even pieces of fish but do not pull apart as the
filling will ooze out.

Bake in 400 degree oven about 20 minutes, until the fish is
flaky and the phyllo dough is golden. Serves 6.

Asparagus and pasta stir fry

8 ounces penne pasta

2 tsp. cooking oil

1 pound asparagus, washed and ends trimmed, sliced into 2" pieces

1 clove garlic, chopped

1 tsp. minced ginger

4 sliced green onions

2 T. low sodium soy sauce

1/8 tsp. dried, crushed red chilies

1 T. toasted sesame seeds

Pinch of sugar

Boil water and cook pasta to personal preference. Drain and set aside, keeping warm.

While pasta is cooking, heat oil in a wok or large frying pan over high heat. Add asparagus, garlic, ginger and green onions, stir frying until asparagus is al dente. Add soy sauce, chilies, sesame seeds and pinch of sugar and continue cooking until all is hot. Add drained pasta, mix thoroughly, serve. Serves 6-8 as a side dish.

GROCERY LIST	(QUANTITY)

FRESH

Asparagus. . . 1 lb. or bundle
Garlic . . . . 1 clove
Ginger root . . . . . . .1 tsp.
Green onions/scallions. . .4

CANS/JARS

Cooking oil . . . . . . .2 tsp.
Vegetable, canola: personal preference
Soy sauce . . . . 2 T.

DRY

Penne pasta . . . . . . .8 oz.

BAKING

Dried red chilies . .1/8 tsp.
Sesame seeds. . . . . . . 1 T.
Sugar . . . . .pinch

Artichoke and mushroom medley

1 pound mushrooms, washed and sliced

1 sweet onion, sliced

4 T. butter

2 14-ounce cans artichoke hearts, rinsed, drained and chopped lightly

½ tsp. freshly ground pepper

¼ tsp thyme

¼ tsp. nutmeg

¼ tsp. white pepper

½ cup dry sherry

Sauté mushrooms and onion in butter until partially cooked, then add artichokes, pepper, thyme, nutmeg and white pepper. Stir. Then add sherry and cook until liquid is reduced. Serves 6-8.

GROCERY LIST	(QUANTITY)
FRESH	
Mushrooms	1 lb.
Onion	1
Sweet	
CANS/JARS	
Artichoke hearts	2
14 oz. cans, in water	
Sherry	½ cup
The drinking kind, not "cooking sherry"	
BAKING	
Black pepper grounds	½ tsp.
Nutmeg	¼ tsp.
Thyme	¼ tsp.
White pepper	¼ tsp.
DAIRY	
Butter	4 T.

Chocolate mousse

6 ounces unsweetened chocolate squares

12 T. butter

6 eggs, separated
(reserve egg whites for a later use)

1 cup brown sugar

2 ½ tsp. cream of tartar

1 cup whipping cream,
avoiding ultra-pasteurized if possible

2 ½ tsp. vanilla

2 T. brandy

Zest of one orange, grated

2 T. almond liqueur

2 T. crème de cacao

¼ cup sugar

Store-bought, decorative cookies

Over a double boiler, melt chocolate and butter together. In medium bowl, beat egg yolks and brown sugar until thick. Combine the egg yolks into chocolate mixture and whisk well and well heated.

Beat whipping cream and cream of tartar until stiff, then fold in chocolate mixture.

(Continued on next page)

GROCERY LIST	(QUANTITY)
FRESH	
Orange	1
DRY	
Cookies	8
Thin, rolled, decorative	
BAKING	
Brown sugar.	1 cup
Cream of tartar. . .	2½ tsp.
Sugar	¼ cup
Chocolate squares . .	6 oz.
Unsweetened	
Vanilla.	2½ tsp.
DAIRY	
Butter.	12 T. (6 oz.)
Eggs	6
Whipping cream. . .	1 cup
NOT ultra pasteurized if possible, difficult to whip into stiff peaks	
MISC. (LIQUOR STORE)	
Almond liqueur.	2 T.
Brandy.	2 T.
Crème de cacao.	2 T.
Ask for the small bottles, (unless larger ones will be consumed) which are usually up front by the registers.	

Combine vanilla, brandy, orange zest, almond liqueur, crème de cacao and sugar. Fold into chocolate mixture. Chill for at least an hour, then spoon into decorative serving dishes (pretty wine glasses with wide openings are recommended.) Chill until ready to serve. Serve with fancy, store-bought decorative cookies placed in each glass-see photo. Makes 8 generous servings – very rich so making 10 means a special treat the next day!

Grocery list PHYLLO-WRAPPED SALMON MENU

FRESH

Asparagus . . . . 1 lb.
Or 1 bundle

Avocadoes. 2
Cilantro . . . . 1 bunch
Garlic . . . . 1 T. + 2 cloves
Ginger root . . . . . . .1 tsp.
Green onions/scallions. . .4
Jalapeno pepper. . . . . . ½
Lemon 1
Limes 4
Medium

Mushrooms . . . . 1 lb.
Onion 1
Sweet

Orange 1
Pine nuts . . . . ¼ cup
Red onion Small . . 1 + ½ cup
Spinach . . . . .6 oz.

CANS/JARS

Artichoke hearts. 2
14 oz. cans, in water

Capers . . . . 1 T.
Cooking oil . . . . . . .2 tsp.
(Vegetable, canola: personal
preference)

Olive oil. . . . . .5 T.
Extra virgin

Kalamata olives . . .11 oz.
(Greek), pitted

Red wine vinegar . . . . 3 T.
Soy sauce . . . . 2 T.
Sun dried tomatoes . . ¼ cup

DRY

Cookies 8
Thin, rolled, decorative

Penne pasta . . . . . . .8 oz.
Tortilla chips . . 13 oz. bag
Flat, round ones

FROZEN

Phyllo dough . . .one package
(Or "filo," should be near the
frozen pie crusts)

Puff Pastry sheets . . 17.3 oz.

MEAT

Bacon . . . . 10 slices
Do not buy microwave
bacon as the fat is needed

Salmon, wild . . . . 1½ lbs.
Or slightly more

Shrimp. . . . . 1 lb.
Uncooked, peeled and
deveined preferable

DAIRY

Blue cheese . . . . . 1 cup
Crumbled

Butter. . . . 12 oz. (3 sticks)
Cream cheese . . . . .8 oz.
Eggs . . . . 7 large

Pesto . . . . .1/3 cup
Prepared basil pesto

Whipping cream. . . 1 cup
NOT ultra pasteurized if possible,
difficult to whip into stiff peaks

BAKING

Brown sugar. . . . . . 1 cup
Chocolate squares . .6 oz.
Unsweetened

Cream of tartar. . . 2½ tsp.
Dried red chilies . . . 1/8 tsp.
Nutmeg . . . . ¼ tsp.
Peppercorns
For grinder + ¾ tsp.

Salt
Salt Kosher . . . . .pinch
Sesame seeds. . . . . . 1 T.
Sugar . . . . . . ¼ cup, ½ tsp.
+ 1 pinch

Thyme . . . . ¼ tsp.
Vanilla . . . . 2½ tsp.
White pepper. . . . . ¼ tsp.

MISC./LIQUOR STORE

Almond liqueur. . . . . . 2 T.
Brandy. . . . . 2 T.
Crème de cacao . . . . 2 T.
Sherry . . . . ½ cup
(The drinking kind,
not "cooking sherry")

Spicy chicken saté with peanut sauce

MENU

Grape and emmenthaler k-bobs

Smoked salmon bruschetta

Roasted corn and pepper salad

Spicy chicken saté with peanut sauce

Cumin glazed carrots

Microwave tomato risotto

Chocolate cranberry espresso torte

Grape & emmenthaler k-bobs

Bunch red grapes
¼ pound Emmenthaler cheese
(or any hard cheese i.e. Gruyere)
Round, wooden toothpicks

Wash grapes and remove from stems. Cube cheese to be small enough to be both bite-sized and a nice base for grape to sit on. Skewer grape first, then cheese, with toothpick, going through until bottom of cheese is reached. Display on serving plate with toothpicks standing up, ready to be taken. This is cute, simple and tasty!

GROCERY LIST	(QUANTITY)
FRESH	
Red grapes. . . large bunch	
Seedless	
DRY	
Toothpicks	
Round, wooden	
DAIRY	
Emmenthaler cheese. . .¼ lb.	
(Or Gruyere)	

Smoked salmon bruschetta

1 baguette cut in ¼ inch slices on the diagonal

1/3 cup walnut oil

4 ounces mascarpone cheese

1 T. Dijon mustard

1 T. capers, drained

4 ounces smoked salmon, cut into slices that would fit nicely on top of toasts

1 avocado, ripe, cut into thin slivers and sprinkled with lemon juice to avoid darkening

1 lemon, zested, then juiced

1/8 + tsp. dried dill

Brush oil on both sides of bread slices and bake in 350 degree oven for 8-10 minutes, until browned. Allow to cool or return to room temperature.

Mix together cheese, mustard, capers, zest and 1/8 tsp. dill. Spread thin layer onto each slice of bread. Layer a slice of salmon and then avocado on top. Sprinkle dill on top.

GROCERY LIST	(QUANTITY)
FRESH	
Avocado	1
Lemon	1
CANS/JARS	
Capers	1 T.
Dijon mustard	1 T.
Walnut oil	1/3 cup
DRY	
Baguette	1
BAKING	
Dill	1/8 tsp.
Plus enough to sprinkle on top	
DAIRY	
Mascarpone cheese	4 oz.
MEAT	
Smoked salmon	4 oz.

Roasted corn and pepper salad

¼ cup extra virgin olive oil

2 T. balsamic vinegar

1 T. sherry

1 T. Dijon mustard

1 tsp. cumin

Salt and pepper to taste

Mix all above ingredients in a small bowl and set aside.
This is your dressing.

4 cups corn, thawed

2 red peppers

2 poblano peppers

½ sweet onion, chopped

**½ - 1 jalapeno (personal preference
– 1 makes this on the spicy side)**

1 cup zucchini, diced

1 cup fresh cilantro, chopped

2 tomatoes, chopped

**2 15.5-oz. cans black beans,
rinsed and drained - optional**

Arrange corn, all peppers (cut in half and seeded, cut side
down) and onion on jellyroll pan, spread out as much as
possible. Spray lightly over all with non-stick cooking spray.
Roast corn, onion and peppers under broiler until skin is dark

(Continued on next page)

GROCERY LIST	(QUANTITY)
FRESH	
Cilantro . . . . .1 bunch	
(Need 1 cup)	
Jalapeno 1	
Poblano peppers. 2	
Red peppers. 2	
Sweet onion medium 1	
Tomatoes 2	
Zucchini. . . . . 1 cup	
CANS/JARS	
Balsamic vinegar . . . . 2 T.	
Black beans 2	
15.5 oz. cans, optional	
Dijon mustard. . . . . . 1 T.	
Olive oil. . . . . ¼ cup	
Extra virgin	
BAKING	
Cumin . . . . 1 tsp.	
Non-stick cooking spray	
Pepper. . . . . to taste	
Salt . . . . to taste	
FROZEN	
Corn kernels. . . . . .4 cups	
MISC.	
Sherry . . . . 1 T.	

and peeling, stirring corn once or twice, then allow to cool.
Peel and chop peppers. In a large bowl, combine corn,
red peppers, poblano peppers, onion, jalapeno, zucchini,
cilantro, tomatoes and beans. Pour dressing over and mix
well, chill for at least an hour before serving. Mix again,
serve. Serves 8.

Spicy chicken saté with peanut sauce

4 tsp. powdered turmeric

1 tsp. salt

2 cups canned, unsweetened coconut milk

4 pounds chicken breasts, skinned and boned, trimmed into 2" cubes

In a large bowl, combine turmeric, salt and coconut milk. Add chicken cubes, tossing to coat well. Cover and refrigerate 1-2 hours.

PREPARE PEANUT SAUCE BELOW.

Drain chicken and thread onto metal skewers or water-soaked bamboo ones. Either cook on hot grill or under broiler, ~2-3 minutes each side. Cut into to be sure there is no pink. Serve on top of couscous or rice, removing skewer in advance. Top with peanut sauce and garnish with cilantro.

PEANUT SAUCE

½" piece fresh ginger root, peeled and minced

1 serrano or jalapeno chili, seeded and minced

1 clove garlic, minced

2 green onions, minced

1/3 cup creamy peanut butter

1/3 cup canned, unsweetened coconut milk

3 T. fresh lemon or lime juice

2 T. fish sauce or soy sauce

1 tsp. sugar to taste

¼ cup chopped fresh cilantro

Mix all in bowl or food processor. Can be made in advance, makes about 1 cup.

GROCERY LIST	(QUANTITY)
FRESH	
Cilantro	¼ cup
Garlic	1 clove
Ginger	½" piece
Scallions	2
Peppers	1
Serrano or jalapeno	
Lemon or lime juice	3 T.
CANS/JARS	
Coconut milk	2 1/3 cups
Unsweetened	
Peanut butter	1/3 cup
Creamy	
Fish sauce	2 T.
(Or soy sauce; Asian section)	
BAKING	
Salt	1 tsp.
Sugar	1 tsp.
Turmeric	4 tsp.
MEAT	
Chicken breasts	4 lbs.
Skinned and boned	
MISC.	
Metal or wooden skewers	

Cumin glazed carrots

2 pounds carrots, cut on the diagonal about ¼ inch thick

4 T. extra virgin olive oil

3 tsp. cumin, ground

2 cups orange juice

Juice of two lemons

2 tsp. honey

½ tsp. kosher salt

¼ tsp. freshly ground black pepper

Sauté carrots in oil with cumin until coated, then add remaining ingredients. Simmer uncovered until liquid has evaporated, 20-30 minutes, stirring occasionally. Serves 8.

GROCERY LIST	(QUANTITY)
FRESH	
Carrots Peeled	2 lb. bag
Lemons	2
CANS/JARS	
Olive oil. Extra virgin	4 T.
Honey	2 tsp.
BAKING	
Cumin Ground	3 tsp.
Kosher salt	½ tsp.
Peppercorns	¼ tsp.
DAIRY	
Orange juice With or without pulp	2 cups

Microwave tomato risotto

1 small onion, chopped

1 tsp. extra virgin olive oil

1 garlic clove, minced

2 cups chicken broth, low sodium, heated to boiling point and kept warm

4 medium tomatoes-on-the-vine, chopped

4 ounces mushrooms, chopped

1 ½ cups Arborio rice

½ cup dry white wine

½ tsp. cumin

½ tsp. coriander

¼ cup Parmesan or Romano cheese, grated

In a 1 ½ quart microwave-safe dish, combine onion, oil and garlic. Cook at 100% power 3 minutes. Add hot broth, tomatoes, rice, wine, cumin and coriander. Cover dish with plastic wrap and cook on full power until liquid is absorbed and rice is tender, about 15 minutes; stirring every 5 minutes. Stir in cheese.

GROCERY LIST	(QUANTITY)
FRESH	
Garlic clove	1
Mushrooms	4 oz.
Onion Small	1
Tomatoes On-the-vine, medium	4
CANS/JARS	
Chicken broth Low sodium	2 cups
Olive oil Extra virgin	1 tsp.
DRY	
Arborio rice (Near regular rice)	1 ½ cups
BAKING	
Coriander	½ tsp.
Cumin	½ tsp.
DAIRY	
Cheese Parmesan or Romano	¼ cup
MISC.	
Dry white wine	½ cup

Chocolate cranberry espresso torte

1 ½ cups fresh cranberries, rinsed

1/3 cup sugar

Zest of one orange

½ tsp. ground coriander

**3 T. crème de cassis,
Chambord or Grand Marnier**

1 1/3 cups semi sweet chocolate chips

8 ounces butter

3 eggs

½ cup sugar

¼ tsp. almond extract

½ cup toasted almonds, ground

1/3 cup flour (plus 1 T. if at high altitude)

1/8 tsp. salt

Combine cranberries, 1/3 cup sugar, orange zest and coriander in a small, covered saucepan and cook over medium heat 5 minutes. Remove from heat and add the liqueur, leave uncovered.

In a double boiler, melt chocolate and butter, remove from heat and set aside.

In a large bowl, beat eggs until frothy, add ½ cup sugar. Add chocolate mixture and blend well.

(Continued on next page)

GROCERY LIST	(QUANTITY)
FRESH	
Cranberries	1½ cups
Mint leaves	1 package
Orange	1
Raspberries	small container
CANS/JARS	
Coffee powder	1½ tsp.
Instant espresso style	
BAKING	
Almonds	½ cup
Almond extract	¼ tsp.
Chocolate	1½ oz.
Unsweetened	
Chocolate chips	1 1/3 cups
Semi sweet	
Coriander Ground	½ tsp.
Flour	1/3 cup
Powdered sugar	1/3 cup
Salt	1/8 tsp.
Sugar	½ + 1/3 cup
Vanilla	½ tsp.
DAIRY	
Butter	8 oz. + 2 T.
Eggs	3
Heavy cream	¼ cup
MISC.	
Crème de cassis	3 T.

Add almond extract and almonds. Add cranberry mixture. Gently fold in flour and salt. Bake at 350 degrees in a greased 9 inch springform pan 40-50 minutes until firm in center. Cool, remove from pan once cooled and place on decorative plate.

ESPRESSO ICING

1/3 cup powdered sugar
1 ½ tsp. instant espresso coffee powder
¼ cup heavy cream
1 ½ ounces unsweetened chocolate
2 T. butter
½ tsp. vanilla

In a medium saucepan, mix together: sugar, coffee and cream. Bring to a boil, then reduce heat and simmer for 5 minutes, stirring occasionally. Add chocolate and mix in, then remove from heat. Blend in butter and vanilla until combined well, then chill until thickened. Drizzle icing over cake until evenly covered, chill until ready to serve. Garnish with mint sprig and fresh raspberries.

Helpful tip: Fresh cranberries are available in the markets during the winter months, so stock up as they freeze beautifully. This is the best way to enjoy them year-round!

Grocery list

FRESH

Avocado 1
Carrots Peeled . . . 2 lb. bag
Cilantro . . . . 1¼ cup
Cranberries . . . . 1½ cups
Garlic . . . . .2 cloves
Ginger. . . . . ½" piece
Jalapenos. 2
Lemons 2
Lemon or lime juice . . . 3 T.
Mint leaves . . . 1 package
Mushrooms . . . . . . .4 oz.
Onion Small 1
Orange 1
Poblano peppers. 2
Raspberries Small container . . 1
Red grapes. 1
Large bunch, seedless
Red peppers. 2
Scallions 2
Sweet onion Medium. . . . 1
Tomatoes Medium 6
Zucchini. . . . . 1 cup

CANS/JARS

Balsamic vinegar . . . . 2 T.
Black beans 2
15.5 oz. cans; optional
Capers . . . . 1 T.
Chicken broth. . . . . 2 cups
Coconut milk . . . 2 1/3 cups
Unsweetened

Coffee powder . . . 1½ tsp.
Instant espresso style
Dijon mustard . . . . 2 T.
Fish sauce Or soy sauce . 2 T.
Olive oil . . ¼ cup, 4T. & 1 tsp.
Extra virgin
Peanut butter . . . .1/3 cup
Creamy
Walnut oil . . . . . 1/3 cup

DRY

Arborio rice . . . . 1½ cups
Baguette 1
Toothpicks Round, wooden

BAKING

Almond extract . . . . ¼ tsp.
Almonds . . . . ½ cup
Chocolate . . . . . 1½ oz.
Unsweetened
Chocolate chips 1 1/3 cups
Semi sweet
Coriander Ground . . .1 tsp.
Cumin Ground . . . . .6 tsp.
Dill . . . . .1/8 tsp.
Plus enough to sprinkle on top
Flour . . . . .1/3 cup
Honey . . . . .3 tsp.
Kosher salt . . . . . . ½ tsp.
Non-stick cooking spray
Peppercorns . . . . . . ¼ tsp.
+ to taste

Powdered sugar . .1/3 cup
Salt . . . 1 1/8 tsp. + to taste
Sugar . . . . ~ ¾ cup
Turmeric. . . . . .4 tsp.
Vanilla . . . . ½ tsp.

DAIRY

Butter. . . . . . . 8 oz. + 2 T.
Eggs 3
Emmenthaler cheese. . . ¼ lb
(Or Gruyere)
Heavy cream . . . . . ¼ cup
Mascarpone cheese . . .4 oz.
Orange juice . . . . . 2 cups
With or without pulp
Parmesan cheese . . ¼ cup
Or Romano

MEAT

Chicken breasts . . . .4 lbs.
Skinned and boned
Smoked salmon . . . . 4 oz.

FROZEN

Corn kernels. . . . . . 4 cups

MISC.

Crème de cassis . . . . . 3 T.
Or Chambord or Grand Marnier
Dry white wine . . . . ½ cup
Metal or wooden skewers
Sherry From liquor store . . . 1 T.

Spicy shrimp over pasta

Hot artichoke spread

Crab-stuffed cherry tomatoes

Spinach, strawberry and feta salad

Spicy shrimp over pasta

Roasted vegetable strudel

Chocolate mint cookies

MENU

Hot artichoke spread

1 (14 oz.) can artichoke hearts, drained, rinsed and chopped
¾ - 1 cup mayo (I use "light")
1 cup grated fresh Parmesan Cheese
½ tsp. garlic powder
Generous dash of fresh lemon juice
Crackers

Combine all ingredients, mixing well. Spoon into lightly greased baking dish. Bake at 350 degrees for 25 minutes. Serve with assorted crackers for dipping.

GROCERY LIST	(QUANTITY)
FRESH	
Lemon	1
CANS/JARS	
Artichoke hearts	1
14 oz. can	
Mayonnaise	¾ - 1 cup
Light or regular	
DRY	
Garlic powder	½ tsp.
Crackers	1 box
Any kind	
DAIRY	
Parmesan cheese . . .	1 cup
Fresh	

Crab stuffed cherry tomatoes

4 T. butter, room temperature

8 ounces cream cheese, room temperature

4 T. low-fat mayonnaise

4 T. minced sweet onion

Juice of ½ lemon

10 ounces cooked crab, chopped

1 ½ tsp. Old Bay seafood seasoning

~50 cherry tomatoes

¼ cup parsley, minced

Combine the butter, cream cheese, mayonnaise, onion, lemon juice, crab and Old Bay. Wash tomatoes and dry. Cut top ¼ off tomato leaving a flat bottom. Scoop or squeeze out insides and turn over to drain on paper towels. Put crab mixture in a plastic baggie, then cut one corner off with a large enough hole to squeeze crab through. Fill the tomatoes with cheese mixture, sprinkle with parsley as garnish, chill.

GROCERY LIST	(QUANTITY)

FRESH
Cherry tomatoes . . . . 50+
Lemon . . . . ½
Parsley. . . . . ¼ cup
Sweet onion . . . . 4 T.

CANS/JARS
Mayonnaise . . . . 4 T.
Low-fat

BAKING
Seafood Seasoning. . . 1½ tsp.
Old Bay brand

DAIRY
Butter. . . . . 4 T.
Cream cheese . . . . . 8 oz.

MEAT
Crab meat . . . . 10 oz.
(No shells)

MISC.
Medium sized plastic bag

Spinach, strawberry & feta salad

¼ cup raspberry vinegar

2 T. balsamic vinegar

1 T. Dijon mustard

1 T. honey

¼ tsp. salt

¼ cup extra virgin olive oil

Mix above ingredients for the dressing and set aside.

15 oz. bag of prewashed baby spinach

1 1/2 cups feta cheese, crumbled

12 oz. fresh strawberries, sliced

¾ cup walnuts, toasted and chopped

In a very large bowl, combine above salad ingredients.
When ready to serve, toss salad with desired amount of
dressing, mixing well. Serves 8.

GROCERY LIST (QUANTITY)

FRESH
Spinach . . . . . 15 oz. bag
Baby spinach, prewashed

Strawberries . . . . . . 12 oz.

CANS/JARS
Balsamic vinegar . . . . 2 T.

Dijon mustard . . . . 1 T.

Olive oil . . . . ¼ cup
Extra virgin

Honey . . . . 1 T.

Raspberry vinegar . . ¼ cup

DRY
Salt . . . . ¼ tsp.

BAKING
Walnuts . . . . ¾ cup

DAIRY
Feta cheese . . . . . 1 ½ cup
Crumbled

Spicy shrimp over pasta

3 lbs. large shrimp, defrosted

4 T. extra virgin olive oil

6 cloves garlic, minced

1 tsp. salt

12 T. butter

**2 tsp. chipotle powder
(chili powder may be substituted)**

4 tsp. freshly ground black pepper

2 2/3 T. Worcestershire sauce

2 T. fresh lemon juice

Wooden or metal skewers

2 Baguettes

Pasta of choice, 2 lbs.

Toss shrimp in a bowl with oil, garlic and 3/4 tsp. salt and set aside to marinate while preparing sauce. Heat butter, chipotle powder, pepper, Worcestershire sauce and ¼ tsp. salt in a small saucepan until butter is melted. Remove from heat and stir in lemon juice.

Begin boiling large pot of salted water for pasta, cook according to directions and personal preference.

Thread shrimp onto skewers lengthwise so that the flat surfaces cook more evenly. Cook over very hot grill for a total of 3-4 minutes. Remove from skewers into bowl, toss with Worcestershire mixture until shrimp are well coated. Serve over pasta on individual plates with baguette. Serves 8.

GROCERY LIST	(QUANTITY)
FRESH	
Garlic cloves	6
Lemon	2 T.
CANS/JARS	
Olive oil. Extra virgin	4 T.
Worcestershire sauce	2 2/3 T.
DRY	
Pasta. Spaghetti, fettuccine, penne, for example	2 lbs.
Baguettes	2
BAKING	
Salt	1+ tsp.
Chipotle powder	2 tsp.
Black pepper Freshly ground	4 tsp.
DAIRY	
Butter	12 T. (¾ cup)
FROZEN	
Shrimp. Peeled and deveined, uncooked	3 lbs.
MISC.	
Metal or wooden skewers	

Roasted vegetable strudel

1 red pepper, cut julienne-style

1 green pepper, cut julienne-style

1 yellow pepper, cut julienne-style

1 onion, sliced

2 zucchini, sliced

3-4 T. extra virgin olive oil

Salt and pepper to taste

Roast above vegetables at 450 degrees for 20 minutes in the olive oil on jellyroll pan, coating well and seasoning with salt and pepper to taste. Let cool.

1 lb. mushrooms

2 T. extra virgin olive oil

Sauté mushrooms in oil until cooked, cool. Strain and add to pepper mixture.

1 box Phyllo dough, defrosted

½ cup sunflower nuts

¼ cup fresh rosemary, minced

¾ lb. butter, melted

(Continued on next page)

GROCERY LIST	(QUANTITY)
FRESH	
Mushrooms	1 lb.
Onion	1
Peppers	1 each
Green, yellow and red	
Rosemary	¼ cup
Zucchini	2
CANS/JARS	
Olive oil	6 T.
Extra virgin	
DRY	
Salt and pepper	to taste
Sunflower nuts	½ cup
DAIRY	
Butter	¾ lb.
FROZEN	
Phyllo dough	1 box

Unroll phyllo dough taking care not to let the pieces dry out.
Place slightly damp towel over the top of the pile, removing
just one sheet at a time. Lightly butter the first three sheets as
one is put over the first. Sprinkle that 3rd sheet with sunflower
nuts and rosemary. Place sheet #4 on top, butter it, then #5,
butter it, then #6. Sprinkle with sunflower nuts and rosemary.
Layer and butter 3 more sheets, with a total of 9. Place a thin
layer of roasted vegetables over the entire dough. Starting
at wider end, roll tightly until the end is reached. Repeat the
steps with remaining phyllo dough and vegetables. Wrap
in parchment and then plastic wrap, chill until ready to use.
Make in advance so that they are allowed to chill, which will
hold them together better. May even be frozen. When ready
to use, slice the rolls on a slight diagonal about 1 inch thick
and place on baking sheet, baking at 450 degrees for 15-
20 minutes, until dough is browned and cooked.

Serves 8 as a side vegetable dish.

Chocolate mint cookies

¾ cup butter

1 ½ cup brown sugar

2 T. water

12 ounces semi sweet chocolate chips

1 tsp. vanilla

2 large eggs

2 ¾ cups flour

½ tsp. salt

1 ¼ tsp. baking soda

1 9.5-oz. bag Andes Mint candies + 10 more mints

In a double boiler, melt together butter, brown sugar and water. Add chocolate chips and stir until melted. Remove from heat and allow to cool, add vanilla. In large mixing bowl, combine eggs, flour, salt and baking soda. Add chocolate mixture and blend completely. Chill dough thoroughly. Meanwhile, remove all mints from wrappers and cut in half, set aside. Roll dough into small balls and place on ungreased baking sheet. Bake at 335 degrees for 7-9 minutes. Remove from oven and place a mint half in the center of cookie. Return to oven for ten seconds to melt chocolate. Remove from oven and swirl melted mint with butter knife. Cool on cooling racks. Makes 70 cookies.

GROCERY LIST	(QUANTITY)
BAKING	
Baking soda	1 ¼ tsp.
Brown sugar	1 ½ cups
Chocolate chips 12 oz. bag, semi sweet	1
Flour All purpose	2¾ cups
Salt	½ tsp.
Vanilla	1 tsp.
DAIRY	
Butter	¾ cup
Eggs	2 large
MISC.	
Andes Mint candies 9.5-oz. bag + 10 more mints, in candy aisle	1

Grocery list SPICY SHRIMP MENU

FRESH

Cherry tomatoes . . . . 50+
Garlic cloves 6
Lemon 3
Mushrooms . . . . . . 1 lb.
Onion 1
Parsley. . . . . ¼ cup
Peppers . . . . .1 each
Green, yellow and red

Rosemary. . . . . ¼ cup
Spinach . . . . .15 oz.
Baby spinach, prewashed

Strawberries. . . . .12 oz.
Sweet onion . . . . 4 T.
Zucchini. 2

CANS/JARS

Artichoke hearts 1
14 oz. can

Balsamic vinegar . . . . 2 T.
Dijon mustard. . . . . . 1 T.
Honey . . . . 1 T.
Mayonnaise . . . ~ 1¼cups
Light or regular

Olive oil. . . . ¾ cup + 2 T.
Extra virgin

Raspberry vinegar. . ¼ cup
Worcestershire sauce. . 2 2/3 T.

DRY

Baguettes. 2
Crackers . . . . 1 box
Any kind

Pasta . . . . .2 lbs.
Spaghetti, fettuccine,
penne for example

BAKING

Baking soda. . . . . 1¼ tsp.
Black pepper . . . . .4 tsp.
Freshly ground

Brown sugar. . . . 1½ cups
Chipotle powder. . . .2 tsp.
Chocolate chips 1
12 oz. bag; semi sweet

Flour . . . . 2¾ cups
All purpose

Garlic powder . . . . ½ tsp.
Salt . . . . 1½ tsp.
Salt and pepper . . to taste
Seafood Seasoning . .1½ tsp.
Old Bay brand

Sunflower nuts . . . . ½ cup
Vanilla. . . . . .1 tsp.
Walnuts . . . . ¾ cup

DAIRY

Butter. . . . . .6½ sticks
Cream cheese . . . . .8 oz.
Eggs . . . . 2 large
Feta cheese . . . . 1½ cup
Crumbled

Parmesan cheese . . . 1 cup
Fresh

MEAT

Crab meat . . . . 10 oz.
No shells

FROZEN

Phyllo dough . . . . . 1 box
Shrimp. . . . . .3 lbs.
Peeled and deveined, uncooked

MISC.

Andes Mint candies. . . . 1
9.5-oz. bag +10 more mints,
in candy aisle

Plastic baggie
Medium sized

Skewers
Metal or wooden

Stuffed pork tenderloin

Apple and parmesan
stuffed mushrooms

Stuffed vienna bread

Caprese salad

Stuffed pork tenderloin

Sautéed carrots and apples
with caraway seeds

Pan-roasted rosemary potatoes

Rum bundt cake

MENU

Apple & parmesan stuffed mushrooms

16 large mushroom caps, washed and dried

1 tart apple (Granny Smith), unpeeled, cut into very small pieces

¼ cup Parmesan cheese, freshly grated

½ cup Italian flavored bread crumbs

1 tsp. garlic powder

2 T. extra virgin olive oil

4 T. butter, divided into 16 slices

Arrange mushroom caps in a baking dish that has been sprayed with cooking spray. Mix together the apple, cheese, bread crumbs, garlic powder and olive oil. Fill each mushroom cap with this mixture, topping with slice of butter. Bake at 350 degrees for 30 minutes, serve hot. Serves 8 people, 2 mushrooms each.

GROCERY LIST	(QUANTITY)
FRESH	
Large mushroom caps (Or mushrooms)	16
Tart apple Such as Granny Smith	1
CANS/JARS	
Olive oil Extra virgin	2 T.
DRY	
Bread crumbs Italian flavored	½ cup
BAKING	
Cooking spray	1 can
Garlic powder	1 tsp.
DAIRY	
Butter	4 T.
Parmesan cheese Block, grated	¼ cup

Stuffed vienna bread

1 loaf unsliced Vienna Bread

1 lb. Swiss cheese, grated

8 oz. fresh mushrooms, coarsely chopped

3 green onions sliced thinly, stems included

2 T. poppy seeds

1 tsp. seasoned salt

1 cup butter

1 ½ tsp. fresh lemon juice

1 T. dry mustard

Score bread by slicing lengthwise to within ½" from bottom in 1" sections. Turn and do the same in the other direction. Stuff bread sections with cheese and mushrooms. Sprinkle scallions, poppy seeds and seasoned salt over top. Melt butter and add lemon juice and dry mustard. Stir to dissolve. Gently spoon butter over bread. Wrap in foil. Bake at 350 for 40 minutes. Fold back foil. Guests can serve themselves by pulling pieces off with a fork. Yield 6-12 servings.

GROCERY LIST	(QUANTITY)
FRESH	
Lemon	1
Mushrooms	8 oz.
Scallions	3
DRY	
Dry mustard	1 T.
Poppy seeds	2 T.
Seasoned salt	1 tsp.
Vienna Bread Unsliced	1 loaf
DAIRY	
Butter	1 cup
Swiss cheese Grated	1 lb.

Caprese salad

8 vine-ripened tomatoes, washed and sliced
8 ounces fresh mozzarella cheese, sliced
Fresh basil leaves, chopped
Aged balsamic vinegar
Peppercorns
Finely ground sea salt, optional

On 8 salad plates, alternate tomato and cheese slices, using an entire tomato for each plate. Sprinkle basil leaves over, then drizzle balsamic vinegar over all. Grind pepper over tops, sprinkle with salt if desired. Serves 8.

It is important to use ripe, flavorful tomatoes, fresh mozzarella and pungent basil leaves as there are few ingredients so each one really needs to hold its own! Also, the aged balsamic will be thicker and sweeter as opposed to regular balsamic, which is very nice for many other recipes. I find mine at our local Farmers' Market and stock up for the winter.

GROCERY LIST	(QUANTITY)

FRESH
Basil . . . . 1 package
Or an entire plant for future use, my recommendation!

Tomatoes 8
Vine-ripened

CANS/JARS
Aged Balsamic vinegar
For drizzling, be sure to buy "aged"

BAKING
Peppercorns
Sea salt
Fine

DAIRY
Mozzarella cheese . . . 8 oz.
Fresh, in water

Stuffed pork tenderloin

Pork Tenderloin
1 sweet onion, large
16 oz. spinach, fresh, chopped
1 clove garlic, minced
½ cup sun dried tomatoes, chopped
1/3 cup black olives, sliced
Salt and pepper to taste
¼ tsp. nutmeg
½ cup Romano or Parmesan cheese, grated
Extra virgin olive oil

Sauté onion and garlic in olive oil until yellow and limp, stirring often. Add desired amount of salt and pepper, then add spinach and cook until limp. Add nutmeg. Remove from heat and add sun dried tomatoes, cheese and olives, mixing well. If planning to use right away, do not cool. If making ahead of time, cool stuffing before placing into pork.

Slice pork tenderloins down the center to about ½" inch from the bottom and open up both sides like a book, laying flat on cutting board. Grind pepper into cavity as well as on outside of meat. Place stuffing inside, tie together with either dental floss or heavy thread to hold stuffing in with sides pulled together. Stuffing will be bulging out the top. Repeat with remaining tenderloins. Gently pat olive oil in palms of hands

(Continued on next page)

GROCERY LIST	(QUANTITY)
FRESH	
Garlic clove	1
Spinach	16 oz.
Sweet onion	1
Large	
CANS/JARS	
Black olives	1/3 cup
Olive oil	
Extra virgin	
Sun dried tomatoes	½ cup
BAKING	
Nutmeg	¼ tsp.
Peppercorns to grind	
Salt	
DAIRY	
Cheese	½ cup
Romano or Parmesan, grated	
MEAT	
Pork Tenderloin	1
Buy largest one possible, often they come 2-4 in a package, allowing them all to be filled and freeze what isn't needed now. Do not buy the flavored ones for this recipe.	
MISC.	
Dental floss or heavy thread	

on outside of meat to brown it nicely once in oven. Carefully
place a meat thermometer in the meat (not stuffing!) and cook
at 375 degrees until it reaches 160 degrees. Once it does,
remove from oven and let it sit for ten minutes before cutting
into 1- inch slices to serve, making certain to keep stuffing on
top of each piece of meat.

Sautéed carrots and apples with caraway seeds

1 pound carrots, sliced
3 medium apples, peeled and sliced
1 ½ T. caraway seeds
2 T. butter

Sauté all ingredients in butter until carrots are al dente. Serve warm. Serves 8.

GROCERY LIST	(QUANTITY)
FRESH	
Apples	3
Medium firm ones	
Carrots	1 lb.
BAKING	
Caraway seeds	1½ T.
DAIRY	
Butter	2 T.

Pan-roasted rosemary potatoes

4 T. butter

4 T. extra virgin olive oil

3 ½ pounds russet potatoes, peeled and cut into cubes

Kosher salt

Peppercorns

Fresh rosemary sprigs, chopped

In a very large sauté pan, melt butter with olive oil. Add potatoes and sauté ten minutes until golden, turning frequently. Turn heat down and cover, cooking another ten minutes. Mix in salt, pepper and rosemary to taste. Transfer to a large baking sheet and bake at 475 degrees about ten minutes, stirring a few times, roasting potatoes until crisp. Serves 8.

Recipe may be prepared several hours before needed and then refrigerated. Bring to room temperature before roasting in oven.

GROCERY LIST	(QUANTITY)
FRESH	
Rosemary	1 bunch
Russet potatoes	3 ½ lbs.
CANS/JARS	
Olive oil	4 T.
Extra virgin	
BAKING	
Kosher salt	to taste
Peppercorns	to taste
DAIRY	
Butter	4 T.

Rum bundt cake

CAKE

½ cup chopped pecans

1 pkg. Yellow cake mix

1 pkg. instant vanilla pudding, 4 oz.

4 eggs

½ cup cold water

½ cup canola oil

½ cup rum

GLAZE

4 T. butter

1/8 cup water

½ cup sugar

¼ cup rum

Preheat oven to 325 degrees. Spray with nonstick spray and flour a bundt pan. Sprinkle pecans over bottom of pan.

Mix all cake ingredients in large, mixing bowl. Pour cake batter over pecans in pan and bake for one hour. Cool on a rack.

Invert cooled cake onto serving plate. Prick top, sides and middle. Drizzle glaze evenly over top.

For Glaze: melt butter in saucepan. Stir in water and sugar. Boil five minutes, stirring occasionally. Stir in rum.

GROCERY LIST (QUANTITY)

CANS/JARS
Canola oil . . . . ½ cup
(Or vegetable oil of choice)

BAKING
Nonstick spray
Pecans. . . . . ½ cup
Sugar . . . . ½ cup
Vanilla pudding 1
4 oz. box; Instant
Yellow cake mix . . . 1 box
Any brand

DAIRY
Butter. . . . . . . 4 T. (¼ cup)
Eggs 4

MISC.
Rum. . . . . ¾ cup

Grocery list

FRESH

Apples. 3
Medium firm ones

Basil . . . . 1 package
Or an entire plant for future use,
my recommendation!

Carrots . . . . 1 lb.

Garlic clove 1

Large mushrooms 16
(For the caps)

Mushrooms . . . . 8 oz.
Any size

Lemon 1

Rosemary. . . . . . 1 bunch

Russet potatoes . . . 3 ½ lbs.

Scallions 3

Spinach . . . . 16 oz.

Sweet onion . . . . . 1 large

Tart apple 1
Such as Granny Smith

Tomatoes 8
Vine-ripened

CANS/JARS

Aged Balsamic vinegar
For drizzling, be sure to buy "aged"

Black olives . . . . . 1/3 cup

Canola oil . . . . ½ cup
(Or vegetable oil of choice)

Olive oil. . . . . . . 6 T. +
Extra virgin

Sun dried tomatoes . . ½ cup

DRY

Dry mustard . . . . 1 T.

Bread crumbs . . . . . ½ cup
Italian flavored

Loaf Vienna Bread
Unsliced

BAKING

Butter. . . . . 1 ¾ cup + 2 T.

Caraway seeds. . . . 1 ½ T.

Garlic powder . . . . . 1 tsp.

Kosher salt . . . . . to taste

Nutmeg . . . . ¼ tsp.

Pecans. . . . . ½ cup

Peppercorns to grind

Poppy seeds. . . . . . . 2 T.

Salt

Sea salt
Fine

Seasoned salt . . . . . 1 tsp.

Sugar . . . . ½ cup

Vanilla pudding . . . 4 oz. box
Instant

Yellow cake mix . . . 1 box
Any brand

DAIRY

Eggs 4

Mozzarella cheese . . 8 oz.
Fresh; in water

Parmesan cheese . . ¼ cup
Block, grated

Romano cheese . . . ½ cup
Or Parmesan; grated

Swiss cheese . . . . . . 1 lb.
Grated

MEAT

Pork Tenderloin . . . . ~5 lbs.
Buy largest one possible, often
they come 2-4 in a package,
allowing you to fill them all and
freeze what you don't need now.
Do not buy the flavored ones for
this recipe.

MISC.

Dental floss
Or heavy thread

Rum. . . . . ¾ cup

Thai-inspired pork k-bobs

MENU

Scallop spinach "sandwiches"

Raspberry brie shells

Jicama and orange salad

Thai-inspired pork k-bobs

Curried green beans and carrots

Nutty wild rice

Simple chocolate cheesecake
with raspberries

Scallop spinach "sandwiches"

SPINACH FILLING

1 T. extra virgin olive oil

¼ cup red onion or sweet onion, minced

2 garlic cloves, minced

4 ounces baby spinach, chopped

¼ cup cream

1 T. freshly grated Parmesan or Romano cheese

1 tsp. dry bread crumbs, unseasoned

1 tsp. nutmeg

¼ tsp. white pepper

1 tsp. freshly ground pepper

SCALLOPS

1 – 1 ½ dozen large scallops, uncooked

1 T. sugar

1 T. salt

1 T. freshly ground pepper

Extra virgin olive oil

Prepare spinach filling first by heating olive oil in a pan, then adding onion and garlic. Add spinach and cook until wilted. Add cream and cook until reduced by half. On low heat, add cheese, bread crumbs, nutmeg and peppers. Let cool.

In a medium bowl, coat scallops with the sugar, salt and

(Continued on next page)

GROCERY LIST	(QUANTITY)
FRESH	
Baby spinach	4 oz.
Garlic cloves	2
Red or sweet onion	¼ cup
CANS/JARS	
Olive oil	~ 2T.
Extra virgin	
DRY	
Bread crumbs	1 tsp.
Unseasoned	
BAKING	
Nutmeg	1 tsp.
Peppercorns	1 1/3 T.
Sugar	1 T.
Salt	1 T.
White pepper	¼ tsp.
DAIRY	
Cheese	1 T.
Parmesan or Romano	
Cream	¼ cup
MEAT	
Scallops	1 – 1½ dozen

pepper. Coat a pan with olive oil and heat, then sauté scallops until golden. Cool.

Heat oven to 375 degrees. Cut each scallop in half horizontally. Place about a teaspoon of the spinach mixture on the bottom half, replace top half to complete "sandwich." Repeat with all scallops, then place them in a baking sheet. Bake 10-12 minutes until hot. Makes 12-18 appetizers; serve with plates and forks.

Raspberry brie shells

**2 packages mini phyllo shells
(30 shells total)**

6 ounces Brie

**1/3 cup raspberry spreadable fruit
(not jam as this has no seeds in it)**

Spread shells out onto a large baking sheet. Cut brie into 30 small pieces and place in shells. Dollop a spoonful of spreadable fruit over brie, dividing the 1/3 cup 30 ways. Bake in a 350 degree oven for 6 minutes, serve.

GROCERY LIST (QUANTITY)

CANS/JARS
Spreadable fruit . . . 1/3 cup
Raspberry; near the jam and jelly

DAIRY
Brie . . . . 6 oz.

FROZEN
Mini phyllo shells 2
Packages of 15 each; found near the puff pastry and pie shells

Jicama and orange salad

5 large oranges

1 small jicama or ½ large one

1 sweet onion

1 bunch cilantro

1/3 cup extra virgin olive oil

¼ cup white wine vinegar

1 tsp. sugar

½ tsp. salt

¼ tsp. either chipotle powder or ancho chili powder

Paprika

Peel and section oranges. Peel and slice jicama, julienne style. Slice onion thinly. Combine all three in a bowl. Using kitchen shears, snip half of the washed cilantro into the bowl, mix. In a separate container, mix oil, vinegar, sugar, salt and chili powder of choice. Pour over orange mixture, serve, sprinkling paprika over for aesthetics. Serves 8.

GROCERY LIST	(QUANTITY)
FRESH	
Cilantro	1 bunch
Jicama Small	1
Oranges	5
Sweet onion	1
CANS/JARS	
Olive oil Extra virgin	⅓ cup
White wine vinegar	¼ cup
BAKING	
Chili powder Chipotle or ancho	¼ tsp.
Paprika	to sprinkle
Salt	½ tsp.
Sugar	1 tsp.

Thai-inspired pork k-bobs

2 pounds pork tenderloin

3 tsp. cumin

3 tsp. coriander

3 tsp. turmeric

3 tsp. garlic, minced

3 tsp. red curry paste

3 tsp. fresh ginger, minced

3 T. brown sugar

3 T. fresh lime juice

14 oz. coconut milk, light

6 T. peanut butter

Cut tenderloin into cubes about 1 inch by 1 inch. Thread onto skewers. In food processor, combine all spices, sugar, lime juice and coconut milk. Mix well. Spoon mixture over k-bobs. Make ahead and store in refrigerator until ready to grill. To remaining sauce, add peanut butter and use as a side sauce to be served with k-bobs. When ready, grill on medium heat so as not to burn sauce, turning as needed.

GROCERY LIST	(QUANTITY)
FRESH	
Garlic	~3 cloves
Ginger root	3 tsp.
Limes	2
CANS/JARS	
Coconut milk	14 oz.
(In Asian foods section) light	
Peanut butter	6 T.
Smooth or chunky	
Red curry paste	3 tsp.
(Check Indian section)	
BAKING	
Brown sugar	3 T.
Coriander	3 tsp.
Cumin	3 tsp.
Turmeric	3 tsp.
MEAT	
Pork tenderloin	2 lbs.

Curried green beans and carrots

1 pound green beans, washed and ends trimmed

½ pound baby carrots, julienne sliced

6 T. butter, room temperature

2 T. curry powder

¼ tsp. salt

¼ tsp. freshly ground pepper

1 lemon, zested

2 lemons, juiced

2 T. brown sugar

1 cup pecans, toasted and chopped

Steam both beans and carrots in steamer pan or in microwave until just tender. Place both in large saucepan. Add in the butter, curry powder, salt, pepper and lemon zest. Heat over low heat while tossing to coat vegetables. Add the lemon juice and brown sugar, stirring until everything is coated and heated. Sprinkle with pecans and serve. Serves 8.

GROCERY LIST	(QUANTITY)
FRESH	
Carrots	½ lb.
Baby carrots, peeled	
Green beans	1 lb.
Lemons	2
BAKING	
Brown sugar	2 T.
Curry powder	2 T.
Pecans	1 cup
Peppercorns	¼ tsp.
Salt	¼ tsp.
DAIRY	
Butter	6 T.

Nutty wild rice

1 cup wild rice, rinsed

5 cups chicken broth

**1 cup pecans or almonds,
coarsely chopped after toasting**

1 cup yellow raisins

Zest of one orange

¼ cup mint leaves, chopped, or 2 T. dried mint

3 scallions, sliced

¼ cup extra virgin olive oil

1/3 cup orange juice with pulp

1 tsp. kosher salt

Freshly ground pepper as desired

Place rice and broth in pan and bring to boil, then simmer for 45 minutes. Drain broth and pour rice into bowl. Add remaining ingredients and mix, adjusting flavors. Prepare at least 2 hours before serving to allow flavors to blend, serve at room temperature. Serves 6-8.

GROCERY LIST	(QUANTITY)
FRESH	
Mint leaves	¼ cup*
Orange	1
Scallions	3
CANS/JARS	
Chicken broth	5 cups
Low sodium if available	
Olive oil	
Extra virgin	
DRY	
Wild rice	1 cup
Uncooked	
BAKING	
Kosher salt	1 tsp.
*Mint	2 T.
(If not using fresh)	
Pecans or almonds	1 cup
Peppercorns	
Yellow raisins	1 cup
DAIRY	
Orange juice	1/3 cup
With pulp	

Simple chocolate cheesecake with raspberries

1 package chocolate wafer cookies

4 T. butter, melted

1 T. sugar

2 8-ounce packages cream cheese, room temperature

2/3 cup sugar

3 eggs, room temperature

1 tsp. vanilla

1 cup whipping cream

2 T. butter, melted

1 12-ounce package Baker's chocolate chips, melted and cooled

Small bag of frozen raspberries, thawed

Spray inside of 9" springform pan and then sprinkle ~ 1 T. sugar inside, shaking around to distribute evenly. In food processor, grind up chocolate wafers and then add 4 T. butter while running. When blended thoroughly, remove and evenly spread into springform pan on bottom and slightly up the sides. In a large mixing bowl using electric mixer, beat cream cheese and sugar until blended. Add eggs, one at a time, vanilla, whipping cream and butter. Mix in melted chocolate and blend well. Pour into prepared springform pan. Bake at 325 degrees for 55 minutes. Place jellyroll pan on the oven

(Continued on next page)

GROCERY LIST	(QUANTITY)
BAKING	
Baker's chocolate chips . . . 12 oz. bag	1
Chocolate wafers . . . . . Package	1
Cooking spray	
Sugar . . 2/3 cup plus 1 T.	
Vanilla . . . . 1 tsp.	
DAIRY	
Butter . . . . 6 T.	
Cream cheese . . . . . . 8-oz. packages	2
Eggs	3
Whipping cream . . . 1 cup	
FROZEN	
Raspberries . . . . Small bag	1

shelf below cheesecake so that any oozing of the cheesecake
from the bottom of the springform pan will be caught. Blend
raspberries in either a blender or food processor until liquefied,
then strain through a metal strainer to separate out the seeds.
Reserve liquid to put aesthetically on each plate, underneath
the piece of cheesecake, when serving.

Grocery List THAI-INSPIRED PORK K-BOBS MENU

FRESH

Baby spinach . . . . . .4 oz.
Carrots . . . . .½ lb.
Baby carrots, peeled
Cilantro . . . . . . .1 bunch
Garlic . . . .~5 cloves
Ginger root
Green beans . . . . . . 1 lb.
Jicama. . . . . 1 small
Lemons 2
Limes. 2
Mint leaves . . . . . ¼ cup*
Orange 6
Red or sweet onion . . ¼ cup
+ 1 sweet onion
Scallions 3

CANS/JARS

Chicken broth. . . . .5 cups
Low sodium if available
Coconut milk . . . . .14 oz.
(In Asian foods section)
Olive oil. . . . . . .~1/2 cup
Extra virgin
Peanut butter . . . . . .6 T.
Smooth or chunky
Spreadable fruit . .1/3 cup
Raspberry; near the jam and jelly
Red curry paste. . . . .3 tsp.
White wine vinegar . . ¼ cup

DRY

Bread crumbs . . . . . . 1 tsp
Unseasoned
Wild rice . . . . 1 cup
Uncooked

MEAT

Pork tenderloin . . . . .2 lbs.
Scallops. . . 1 – 1½ dozen

BAKING

Baker's chocolate chips . 1
12 oz. bag
Brown sugar. . . . . . . .5 T.
Chili powder . . . . . ¼ tsp.
Chipotle or ancho
Chocolate wafers 1
Package
Cooking spray
Coriander . . . . .3 tsp.
Cumin . . . . .3 tsp.
Curry powder. . . . . . .2 T.
Kosher salt
*Mint . . . . 2 T.
If not using fresh
Nutmeg. . . . . .1 tsp.
Paprika . . . . . to sprinkle
Pecans. . . . . 1 cup
(See next item)
Pecans or almonds . . .1 cup

DRY

Peppercorns . . . .~2 T.
Salt . . . . . . 1 T. + ¾ tsp.
Sugar . . . . .2/3 cup
Plus 2 T. plus 1 tsp.
Turmeric. . . . . .3 tsp.
Vanilla . . . . .1 tsp.
White pepper. . . . . ¼ tsp.
Yellow raisins . . . . . 1 cup

DAIRY

Brie. . . . . .6 oz.
Butter. . . . 12 T. (1½ sticks)
Cream . . . . ¼ cup
Cream cheese 2
8-oz.packages
Eggs 3
Orange juice . . . .1/3 cup
With pulp
Cheese . . . . 1 T.
Parmesan or Romano
Whipping cream. . . 1 cup

FROZEN

Mini phyllo shells 2
Packages of 15 each; found near
the puff pastry and pie shells
Raspberries 1
Small bag

Vegetarian roasted red pepper lasagna

MENU

Tortilla roll-ups

Spinach artichoke dip

Mandarin orange and spinach salad

Vegetarian roasted red pepper lasagna

Beet greens and garbanzo beans

Roasted cauliflower

Baked alaska

Tortilla roll-ups

2 8-ounce packages cream cheese, softened

1 package (1.6 ounces) ranch dressing mix

8 flour or flavored tortillas

6 green onions, minced

2 4-ounce cans chopped green chilies, drained

2 4-ounce cans black olives, chopped, drained

1 red bell pepper, minced

**¼ pound sharp Cheddar cheese,
shredded (1 cup)**

Mix cream cheese and ranch dressing mix in food processor until smooth. Spread mixture over tortillas. Sprinkle onions, chilies, olives, pepper and cheese over top and roll tightly. Wrap rolled tortillas in plastic wrap and chill at least 2 hours or overnight.

To serve, unwrap and slice into 1-inch spirals.

GROCERY LIST (QUANTITY)

FRESH

Red bell pepper 1

Scallions/green onions . . . 6

CANS/JARS

Black olives 2
Pitted, 4-oz. cans

Green chilies 2
Chopped, 4-oz. cans

DRY

Flour tortillas. 8
Any color

Ranch dressing mix . . . 1.6 oz.
Hidden Valley, envelope

DAIRY

Cheddar cheese . . . . ¼ lb.
Shredded

Cream cheese 2
8-oz. Packages

Spinach artichoke dip

Frozen spinach, 16 ounces, thawed and drained

Artichokes – 2 14-ounce cans, rinsed

Water chestnuts, 8 ounces, diced

Hidden Valley Dip Mix powder 1 oz. envelope

Sweet onion, ½, chopped

8 ounces light sour cream

¾ cup light mayonnaise

½ tsp. white pepper

¼ tsp. nutmeg

Mix all ingredients together, chill, serve with crackers and vegetables to dip.

GROCERY LIST	(QUANTITY)
FRESH	
Dipping vegetables	
Onion	½
Sweet	
CANS/JARS	
Artichokes	2
14 oz. cans, in water	
Mayonnaise	¾ cup
Light	
Water chestnuts	1
8-oz. can	
DRY	
Dip Mix	1 oz.
Hidden Valley, envelope	
Nutmeg	¼ tsp.
White pepper	½ tsp.
DAIRY	
Sour cream	8 oz.
Light	
FROZEN	
Spinach	16 oz.

Mandarin orange & spinach salad

SALAD

3 T. sugar

1 lb. baby spinach, fresh

5 scallions, sliced

2 small cans mandarin oranges

½ cup almonds, toasted in sugar above

DRESSING

6 T. sugar

6 T. white vinegar

¾ cup oil
(or extra virgin olive oil, recommended)

1 ½ tsp. salt or less

Dash pepper

Mix dressing. Toss salad ingredients in large bowl while mixing dressing in. Serve fairly quickly.

GROCERY LIST	(QUANTITY)
FRESH	
Baby spinach	1 lb.
Scallions	5
CANS/JARS	
Mandarin oranges . . . . Small cans	2
Oil of choice	¾ cup
White vinegar	6 T.
BAKING	
Almonds . . . . Sliced	½ cup
Pepper.	dash
Salt	1 ½ tsp.
Sugar	9 T.

Vegetarian roasted red pepper lasagna

4 red peppers, roasted, peeled
1 T. extra virgin olive oil
1 28-ounce can chopped tomatoes
¼ cup fresh parsley, minced
4 garlic cloves, minced
½ tsp. ground peppercorns
1/3 cup butter
½ cup flour
½ tsp. salt
½ tsp. nutmeg (fresh, grated, if possible)
3 cups 2% milk
16 ounce box lasagna noodles
2 cups mozzarella cheese, grated

Once peppers have cooled and have been peeled, cut julienne-style and cook in olive oil in large saucepan. Stir in tomatoes (do not drain!), parsley, garlic and ground pepper. Bring to a boil, then reduce heat and simmer for 20 minutes, stirring occasionally. Set aside.

While red sauce is simmering, prepare white sauce. Melt butter in saucepan, then add flour, whisking constantly until smooth. Add salt and nutmeg. Then whisk in milk and cook until thickened over medium heat, taking care not to allow it to boil over. Set aside. Prepare lasagna noodles according to directions but do not

(Continued on next page)

GROCERY LIST	(QUANTITY)
FRESH	
Garlic	4 cloves
Parsley.	¼ cup
Red peppers	4
CANS/JARS	
Tomatoes	1
28 oz. can, chopped	
Olive oil.	1 T.
Extra virgin	
DRY	
Lasagna	16 oz. box
BAKING	
Flour	½ cup
Nutmeg	½ tsp.
Peppercorns	½ tsp.
Salt	½ tsp.
DAIRY	
Butter.	1/3 cup
Milk, 2%	3 cups
Mozzarella cheese. . .	2 cups
Grated	

overcook as they will cook in the oven. Drain and rinse in cold water. Butter the bottom of a 9x13" glass baking dish and cover bottom with layer of noodles. Spread 1/3 of the pepper sauce over the noodles, then spread ¼ of the white sauce over. Sprinkle ¼ of the mozzarella cheese over top. Repeat two more times. End with noodles, white sauce and mozzarella cheese. Bake at 350 degrees for 35 minutes/ until bubbly around edges and light brown on top. Allow to rest ten minutes before serving. Serves 10-12.

Beet greens & garbanzo beans

2 T. extra virgin olive oil

2 cloves garlic, chopped

16 ounces beet greens, chopped

¼ tsp. coriander

½ tsp. paprika

½ cup vegetable broth

2 tsp. balsamic vinegar

15.5 ounce can garbanzo beans, rinsed and drained

1 tsp. kosher salt

Pepper to grind

Heat olive oil in a very large sauté pan. Add garlic and brown, then add beet greens and stir, cover until limp. Add coriander and paprika. Then add vegetable broth and balsamic vinegar, heating and mixing well with greens. Add garbanzo beans, salt and pepper. Heat thoroughly.

GROCERY LIST (QUANTITY)

FRESH

Beet greens . . . . . .16 oz.
Save the beets for another recipe-separate and weigh at the market, if possible.

Garlic cloves 2

CANS/JARS

Balsamic vinegar . . .2 tsp.
Garbanzo beans 1
(Chick peas) 15.5 oz. can

Olive oil. . . . . .2 T.
Extra virgin

Vegetable broth . . . ½ cup
Low sodium

BAKING

Coriander . . . . ¼ tsp.
Kosher salt . . . . .1 tsp.
Paprika . . . . ½ tsp.
Peppercorns to grind

Roasted cauliflower

1 large head cauliflower trimmed of leaves and washed

Extra virgin olive oil

Kosher salt

Peppercorns

Garlic powder

Paprika

Place cauliflower head in a round, glass oven-proof dish and brush generously with olive oil. Then sprinkle on salt, pepper, garlic powder and paprika. Gently pull florets apart so flavors can ooze into the center. Place in middle of oven and cook at 350 degrees for 35 minutes. Tips will be browned. Remove from oven, brush once more with oil and spice drippings from pan, then cut cauliflower apart and serve.

I found my cauliflower at our local Farmers' Market and it was very sweet and flavorful.

GROCERY LIST	(QUANTITY)
FRESH	
Cauliflower head 1	
Large	
CANS/JARS	
Olive oil	
Extra virgin; Enough to brush	
BAKING	
Kosher salt	
Enough to sprinkle over	
Peppercorns	
Enough to sprinkle over	
Garlic powder	
Enough to sprinkle over	
Paprika	
Enough to sprinkle over	

Baked alaska

This is a really fun and easy dessert but must be made at least the day before!

1 box favorite cake mix*

1.5 quarts favorite ice cream that will complement the ice cream*

5 egg whites

¼ tsp. cream of tartar

1 cup sugar

½ tsp. vanilla

1/4 cup rum or brandy must be 120-130 proof, no less

Mix cake according to directions BUT bake it on a jellyroll pan lined with parchment paper and sprayed with non-stick cooking spray. Bake it at 400 degrees for about 18 minutes, until baked through. Cool.

Take ice cream out of freezer and allow to soften while next step is being prepared.

Using a 1.5 liter bowl as a stencil, trace a circle on the cake and cut it with knife. Trace another one but cut it an extra half inch larger. Cut out with knife. Place larger of two cake circles into plastic lined bowl, pressing cake into the gaps.

(Continued on next page)

GROCERY LIST	(QUANTITY)
BAKING	
Cake mix	
Any flavor	
Cream of tartar	¼ tsp
Sugar	1 cup
Vanilla	½ tsp.
DAIRY	
Eggs	5 whites
FROZEN	
Ice cream	1.5 quarts
MISC.	
Rum or brandy	¼ cup
120-130 proof	
Plastic wrap	
Enough to line bowl	

Possible combinations- chocolate cake & coffee ice cream, German chocolate cake with coconut ice cream, basic chocolate and vanilla combo, spice cake with pumpkin ice cream.

Empty softened ice cream into bowl, pressing down. Level off ice cream in bowl, then place smaller cake circle on top and press down firmly. Cover bowl and freeze until next day.

Preheat oven to 500 degrees. Whip egg whites with cream of tartar until stiff peaks appear. Add sugar and vanilla and continue to beat until stiff and glossy. Quickly remove cake from freezer and place on baking tray. Cover thoroughly with meringue forming irregular peaks. Bake cake for 5-8 minutes or until lightly browned-watch carefully as ovens vary and it is very easy to burn! Remove from oven and slide onto platter that can handle the heat of the fire. Turn lights off, ignite rum and pour over cake. Make grand presentation to guests with flaming dessert! Fire will not last long so haste is important!

Grocery list VEGETARIAN LASAGNA MENU

FRESH

Baby spinach . . . 1 lb. bag

Beet greens . . . . . . 16 oz.
Save the beets for another recipe-separate and weigh at the market, if possible.

Cauliflower head . . .1 large

Dipping vegetables for dip

Garlic . . . . .6 cloves

Onion . . . . ½
Sweet

Parsley. . . . . ¼ cup

Red bell peppers. 5

Scallions/green onions . . 11

CANS/JARS

Artichokes 2
14 oz. cans; in water

Balsamic vinegar . . .2 tsp.

Black olives 2
Pitted, 4-oz. cans

Garbanzo beans. 1
(Chick peas) 15.5 oz. can

Green chilies 2
4-oz. cans; chopped

Mandarin oranges 2
Small cans

Mayonnaise. . . . . . ¾ cup
Light

Oil of choice . . . . . ¾ cup

Olive oil. . . . . .3 T +
Extra virgin

Tomatoes . . . . .28 oz. can
Chopped

Vegetable broth . . . ½ cup
Low sodium

Water chestnuts 1
8- oz. can

White vinegar . . . . . . 6 T.

DRY

Dip mix . . . 1 oz. envelope
Hidden Valley brand

Flour tortillas. 8
Any color

Ranch dressing mix . .1.6 oz.
Hidden Valley brand envelope

Lasagna. . . . . .16 oz. box

BAKING

Almonds . . . . ½ cup
Sliced

Cake mix
Any flavor, for Baked Alaska

Coriander . . . . ¼ tsp.

Cream of tartar. . . . .¼ tsp

Flour . . . . ½ cup

Garlic powder

Kosher salt . . . . . . .1 tsp.
+ enough to sprinkle

Nutmeg . . . . ¾ tsp.

Paprika . . . . ½ +

Peppercorns to grind . . ½ tsp.

Salt . . . . .2 tsp.

Sugar . . . . . 1 cup + 9 T.

Vanilla. . . . . ½ tsp.

White pepper. . . . . ½ tsp.

DAIRY

Butter. . . . . .1/3 cup

Cheddar cheese . . ¼ lb.
Shredded

Cream cheese 2
8-oz. packages

Eggs . . . . .5 whites

Milk, 2% . . . . 3 cups

Mozzarella cheese. . .2 cups
Grated

Sour cream, light . . .8 oz.

FROZEN

Ice cream. . . . . 1.5 quarts
for Baked Alaska

Spinach. . . . . .16 oz.

MISC.

Plastic wrap
Enough to line bowl

Rum or brandy . . . . ¼ cup
120-130 proof

Yellowfin tuna atop a bed of sautéed spinach

MENU

Blue cheese and bacon dates

Brie and pesto appetizer

Curried butternut squash soup with apples

Yellowfin tuna atop a bed of sautéed spinach

Spring vegetable risotto

Cheddar popovers

Nutty pumpkin pie

Blue cheese and bacon dates

10 ounces pitted dates

4 ounces crumbled blue cheese

2.1 ounces precooked, microwave bacon, cut in half *

Widen openings on ends of dates with small finger or kitchen utensil. Using hands, stuff with blue cheese. Wrap a piece of bacon around date, secure with toothpick. Bake at 400 degrees for 3 minutes. *Bacon is optional as these are very good without it. If it is omitted, warming up is optional.

GROCERY LIST	(QUANTITY)

FRESH/DELI
Blue cheese . . . . 4 oz.
Crumbled

BAKING
Dates. . . . . 10 oz.
Pitted

MEAT
Bacon . . . . 2.1 oz.
Microwave type, precooked

MISC.
Toothpicks
Rounded

Brie and pesto appetizer

**Brie – 1 pound wheel
or smaller if larger is not available**
Pesto – store bought
Crackers
Apples

Slice brie horizontally and remove top, set aside. Scoop enough pesto onto bottom half to cover to edges and so that it is about ¼"-½" thick. Replace top onto pesto and place the brie in a glass pie dish that is just slightly larger than the brie. Heat oven to 350 degrees. When it reaches that temperature, turn oven off and place brie inside. Let it bake for 30-45 minutes, remove and serve with crackers and sliced apples. The pesto will ooze out the sides and the brie will be a perfect spreading consistency.

Leftover tip – toss brie and pesto with bowl of hot pasta and serve as a meal.

GROCERY LIST	(QUANTITY)
FRESH	
Apples	3
Tart	
DRY	
Crackers	1 box
Any kind	
DAIRY	
Brie wheel	
Choose size to fit the needs for the number entertaining	
Pesto	
Prepared, large enough container to be able to spread pesto about ¼" thick onto brie half	

Curried butternut squash soup with apples

1 butternut squash

1 large onion, peeled and quartered

1 medium head of garlic, unpeeled

6 cups chicken broth, low sodium

2 tsp. ginger root, chopped

1 T. curry powder

1 bay leaf

½ tsp. oregano

½ tsp. cinnamon

¼ tsp. nutmeg

Peppercorns to taste

2 hard apples, peeled and cubed

1 Baguette

Heat oven to 375 degrees. Cut squash in half and seed, place cut side down on sprayed baking sheet along with onion chunks. Wrap garlic head in foil and put on sheet. Bake for 45 minutes until squash is very soft. Cool, then scoop pulp out and put into bowl of food processor along with onions. Next squeeze garlic cloves out of skins and add to food processor. Puree until smooth.

In a large dutch oven, add squash mixture, broth, ginger, curry, bay leaf, oregano, cinnamon, nutmeg and pepper. Bring to boil, reduce heat and simmer for 15 minutes.

(Continued on next page)

GROCERY LIST	(QUANTITY)
FRESH	
Apples.	2
Hard ones	
Butternut squash	1
Garlic	1 head
Medium	
Ginger root	.2 tsp.
Onion	1
Large	
CANS/JARS	
Chicken broth.	6 cups
Low sodium (48 ounces)	
BAKING	
Bay leaf.	1
Cinnamon	½ tsp.
Curry powder.	1 T.
Non-stick baking spray	
Nutmeg	¼ tsp.
Oregano	½ tsp.
Peppercorns to grind	
MISC.	
Baguette	1

Into 8 serving bowls, place equal amounts of apple cubes into each one. Pour soup over top, making sure to discard bay leaf before it lands in a bowl! The apples make a nice surprise once the bottom is reached. Serve with a baguette. Serves 8.

Yellowfin tuna atop a bed of sautéed spinach

8 Yellowfin tuna steaks, sushi grade
Pepper grounds, 5 peppercorn blend
Garlic powder
Dehydrated onions
Butter
20 ounces baby spinach
¼ cup Pine nuts, toasted
Soy sauce to taste
Wasabi to taste – mix with water
Ginger, fresh, to taste

Press pepper, garlic and onion onto both sides of tuna. Heat butter in large frying pan until slightly dark. Blacken on each side for 30 seconds. Remove from heat and let sit covered for another 2 minutes. Meanwhile, heat skillet with 2 T. olive oil and sauté spinach until limp. Season with white pepper, add toasted pine nuts. Slice thinly and serve over sautéed spinach with soy, ginger and wasabi mixed in small ramekins. Serves 8.

GROCERY LIST	(QUANTITY)
FRESH	
Baby spinach	2
10-oz. bags	
Ginger root	
Pine nuts	¼ cup
CANS/JARS	
Olive oil	2 T.
Extra virgin	
Soy sauce	
Low sodium is good	
BAKING	
Dehydrated onions	
Garlic powder	
Peppercorns	
Wasabi powder	
DAIRY	
Butter	
MEAT	
Yellowfin tuna steaks	8
Sushi grade	

Spring vegetable risotto

1 14-ounce can quartered artichokes, rinsed and drained

1 lemon and zest

2 T. extra virgin olive oil

¼ pound pearl onions, peeled

2 garlic cloves, minced

3 cups prepared chicken stock

Sea or kosher salt and peppercorns to taste

1 ½ pounds sugar snap peas

½ pound asparagus, cut into one inch pieces

1 cup fresh or frozen peas (defrosted)

1 ½ cups Arborio rice

2 T. butter

1 cup Parmesan or Romano cheese, freshly grated

¼ cup parsley, chopped

In a small bowl, mix artichoke hearts with lemon juice and zest. Heat olive oil in large sauté pan and add artichokes, onions and garlic, sauté until warm, stirring often. Add ½ cup of the stock along with a pinch of salt and cover, reducing heat and cooking for ten minutes. Uncover and simmer until most of the liquid has evaporated.

(Continued on next page)

GROCERY LIST	(QUANTITY)
FRESH	
Asparagus	½ lb.
Garlic cloves	2
Lemon	1
Parsley	¼ cup
Peas	1 cup
(Unless frozen is preferred)	
Pearl onions	¼ lb.
Sugar snap peas	1 ½ lb.
CANS/JARS	
Artichokes	14 oz. can
Quartered	
Chicken stock	3 cups
Olive oil	2 T.
Extra virgin	
DRY	
Arborio rice	1 ½ cups
BAKING	
Peppercorns	
Sea or kosher salt	
DAIRY	
Butter	2 T.
Cheese	1 cup
Parmesan or Romano	

Prepare a large steamer pot and place snap peas, asparagus and peas in steamer, "blanch" for 5 minutes, drain and set aside.

In a 3rd saucepan, bring remaining 2 ½ cups stock to a simmer.

Add the rice to the artichokes mixture and stir over medium heat, uncovered, 3 minutes or until rice is transparent. Add a ladle-full of stock at a time, stirring well after each addition. Only add more when last ladle-full has been absorbed, keeping grains moist. This is important to obtain a creamy texture so do not add all the stock at once. This process will take 18 – 22 minutes. Then add the snap peas, asparagus, peas, butter, parsley and cheese. Continue stirring until warm. Serves 8 as a side dish.

Cheddar popovers

1 cup flour (+ 2 T. if at high altitude)
¼ tsp. salt
1 cup non-fat milk
2 eggs
½ cup cheddar cheese, grated
Dash of paprika

Preheat oven to 375 degree. Mix flour and salt. Add milk and eggs and beat one minute on high with electric mixer. Stir in cheese and paprika. Spray 12 muffin cups with non-stick spray and fill each half-full with batter. Bake 35-40 minutes. Remove from oven to cut a slit into the side of each one and then bake 5 minutes longer. Remove from pans and serve warm. May be frozen and reheated. Makes about 8 popovers.

GROCERY LIST	(QUANTITY)
BAKING	
Flour	1 cup + 2 T.
Paprika	dash
Salt	¼ tsp.
DAIRY	
Cheddar cheese Grated	½ cup
Eggs	2
Non-fat milk	1 cup

Nutty pumpkin pie

PIE CRUST

1 ¼ cups flour

1/3 cup powdered sugar

1/3 teaspoon salt

½ teaspoon cinnamon

1/3 pecans, toasted

9 tablespoons butter, cut into smaller chunks

¼ cup butter, melted

¼ cup brown sugar

½ cup pecans, chopped and toasted

Water if needed

PIE

2 cups pumpkin, canned

1 cup brown sugar

4 eggs

1/3 cup rum

1 ¼ cups heavy cream

3 tablespoons crystallized ginger, coarsely chopped

1 tablespoon cinnamon

½ tsp. ginger

½ tsp. cloves

½ tsp. allspice

¼ tsp. nutmeg

¼ tsp. salt

(Continued on next page)

GROCERY LIST	(QUANTITY)
BAKING	
Allspice	½ tsp.
Brown sugar	1¼ cups
Cinnamon	1 T. + ½ tsp.
Cloves	½ tsp.
Crystallized ginger	3 T.
Flour	1¼ cups
Ginger	½ tsp.
Nutmeg	¼ tsp.
Pecans	½ cup + 1/3 cup
Powdered sugar	1/3 cup
Pumpkin	2 cups
(100% pumpkin, not pie filling)	
Salt	1/3 tsp.+ ¼ tsp.
DAIRY	
Butter	¾ cup + 1 T.
Eggs	4
Heavy cream	1¼ cups
MISC.	
Rum	1/3 cup

In a food processor, whirl together flour, sugar, salt, cinnamon and pecans. Add 9 T. butter and pulse until it is mixed well. Add 2 tsp. water, mix, add more if necessary to hold together. Knead dough with hands, chill for an hour. Roll on floured board until it will fit nicely into a deep, 10" pie dish. Poke small holes in bottom of crust. Into bottom, place mixture of melted butter, brown sugar and pecans. Bake for 5 minutes at 425 degrees. Lower oven temperature to 350.

Combine in a large bowl pumpkin, brown sugar, eggs, rum, cream, crystallized ginger, cinnamon, ginger, cloves, allspice, nutmeg and salt. Once mixed well, pour into prepared crust and bake for 40 – 50 minutes. Cool before serving.

Grocery list YELLOWFIN TUNA MENU

FRESH

Apples. 5
Tart, hard ones

Asparagus . . . . ½ lb.

Baby spinach 2
10-oz. bags

Butternut squash 1

Garlic . . . . 1 head
+ 2 cloves, medium

Ginger root . . . . . 2 tsp. +

Lemon 1

Onion . . . . 1 large

Parsley. . . . . ¼ cup

Pearl onions . . . . . . ¼ lb.

Peas . . . . 1 cup
(Unless frozen is preferred)

Pine nuts . . . . ¼ cup

Sugar snap peas. . . 1½ lb.

CANS/JARS

Artichokes . . . . 14 oz. can
Quartered

Chicken broth. . . . . 6 cups
Low sodium (48 ounces)

Chicken stock . . . . . 3 cups

Olive oil Extra virgin . . . 4 T.

Soy sauce

DRY

Arborio rice . . . . 1½ cups
(Near rice)

Crackers . . . . 1 box
Any kind

MEAT

Bacon . . . . 2.1 oz.
Microwave type, precooked

Yellowfin tuna steaks . . . 8
Sushi grade

MISC.

Baguette 1

Rum. . . . . .1/3 cup

Toothpicks Rounded

BAKING

Allspice . . . . ½ tsp.

Bay leaf. 1

Brown sugar. . . . 1¼ cups

Cinnamon . . . 1 T. + 1 tsp.

Cloves . . . . ½ tsp.

Crystallized ginger . . . 3 T.

Curry powder. . . . . . 1 T.

Dates Pitted . . . . . .10 oz.

Dehydrated onions

Flour . . . . .2¼ cups + 2 T.

Garlic powder

Ginger. . . . . ½ tsp.

Non-stick baking spray

Nutmeg . . . . ½ tsp.

Oregano . . . . ½ tsp.

Paprika . . . . dash

Pecans. . ½ cup + 1/3 cup

Peppercorns 5
Peppercorn blend

Powdered sugar . .1/3 cup

Pumpkin. . . . . .2 cups
(100% pumpkin, not
pumpkin pie filling)

Salt . . . .1/3 tsp. + ½ tsp.

Sea or kosher salt

Wasabi powder
(May be in Asian section)

DAIRY

Blue cheese . . . . . . .4 oz.
Crumbled

Brie wheel
Choose size to fit the needs
for the number entertaining*

Butter. . . . . ¾ cup + 3 T. +

Cheese Cheddar. ½ cup (~2 oz.)

Eggs 6

Heavy cream . . . 1¼ cups

Non-fat milk . . . . . . 1 cup

Cheese . . . . 1 cup
Parmesan or Romano

Pesto* . . . . prepared
Large enough container to be
able to spread pesto about ¼"
thick onto brie

Useful information AND HELPFUL HINTS

Have you ever run out of baking powder in the middle of a recipe?

Well, here's what you do to substitute: mix a ratio of 2:1 cream of tartar to baking soda. Use the required amount the recipe calls for of baking powder using this mixture and you will be set!

Butter – 4 ounces = 8 tablespoons = ½ cup= 1 stick

Ever need buttermilk or sour milk and forget to buy it?

Use 1 teaspoon of white vinegar in a cup of milk and mix. That will do the trick.

Ever wonder what the dry weight equivalent is of chocolate chips when a recipe calls for a certain amount?

I have used this one a lot. 6 ounces of chocolate chips = 1 cup chocolate chips.

Ever wonder how many tablespoons are in a liquid cup?

This is useful to know: 8 liquid ounces will equal 16 liquid tablespoons.

Peppercorns are so flavorful that ground pepper should be avoided if at all possible.

Invest in any kind of pepper grinder. Purchase a blend of peppercorns: black, red, green and white. Mix in equal parts.

Additional tip: in a mortar with pestle, grind slightly some whole allspice and add to the peppercorns in the grinder. The flavor is so good. Peppercorns can usually be found at natural food stores and naturally, specialty spice stores.

Tired of burning simple rice?

An electric rice maker is a must! Years ago I only saw them at Asian grocery stores but now they can be found anywhere kitchen appliances are sold. And the price is very reasonable. Use the ratio of 1 part rice to 2 parts liquid and it will be perfect every time… except at higher elevations, where I add an extra ¼ cup liquid (water or broth.)

Not sure how to "roast" a pepper?

There are several ways but this is the easiest one I have found. Spray a large jellyroll pan with non-stick cooking spray. Set oven rack very high but not so high peppers on tray will touch burners. Turn on broiler. Wash, dry and slice peppers in half lengthwise, discarding seeds and stem. Place cut-side down on sheet and place in oven once hot. Broil and check every few minutes until they are nicely charred and the skin is blistered. It may be necessary to move sheet a couple of times to char evenly but it is not necessary to roast 100%. Remove from

oven and place in a paper bag or under loose tent of foil until cooled. Then gently peel off the roasted skin and discard. Use pepper according to recipe. This is actually all very easy and so worth the trouble given the delicious flavor. (Roasting may also be accomplished on a grill and on a gas burner.)

A food scale is a must and very inexpensive to purchase. Once it is a fixture in the kitchen, it will be used more than imagined.

Confused about how to "toast" nuts?

Place nuts evenly in a small frying pan. DO NOT OIL OR SPRAY THE PAN as the nuts have plenty of oil themselves. Turn burner on to almost high and heat the nuts, turning often until they are toasted but not burned. Do not walk away from this as they will burn very quickly! Trust me on this one.

Another favorite and a "must have" is a **zester** (p.198). After years of grating my lemon rinds on the smaller side of the grater, which is no fun to clean out, I discovered this handy little tool. No more messy grater and raw knuckles! It is also inexpensive and will be used a lot.

Index BY CATEGORY & ALPHABETICAL LISTING

(ITEMS IN **BOLD** PRINT HAVE BEEN PHOTOGRAPHED)

Index _(CONTINUED)

(ITEMS IN **BOLD** PRINT HAVE BEEN PHOTOGRAPHED)

Index (CONTINUED)

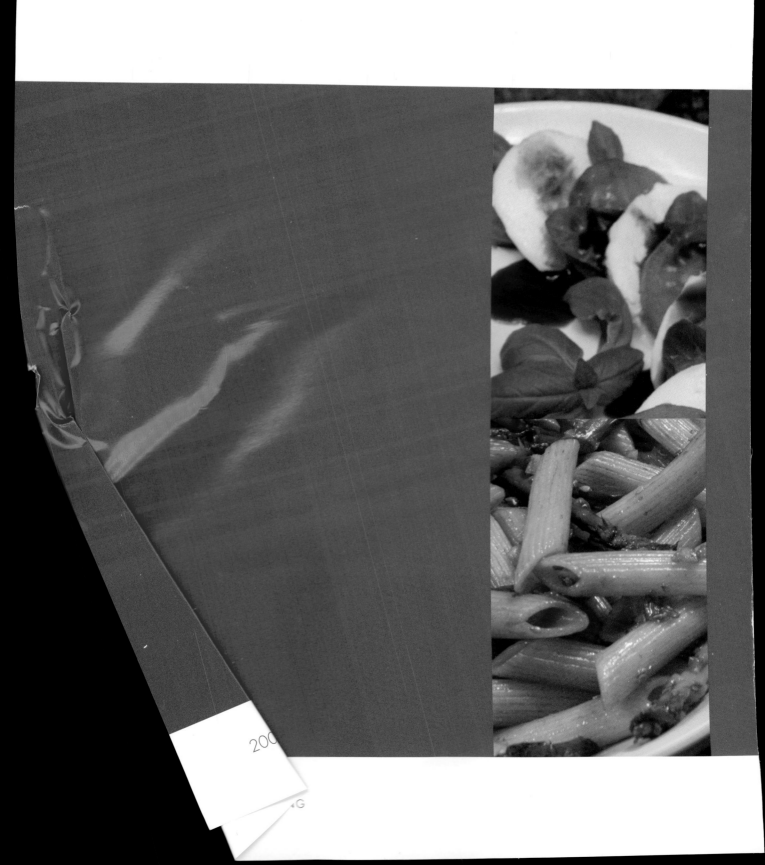